THE CREATIVE YEARS

The Creative Years

Reuel L. Howe

A Crossroad Book
THE SEABURY PRESS
NEW YORK

The Seabury Press
815 Second Avenue
New York, N.Y. 10017

© 1959 by The Seabury Press, Inc.
Designed by P. Atkinson Dymock
Printed in the United States of America

Twenty-second Printing

Library of Congress Catalog Card Number: 59-6166

ISBN: 0-8164-2012-2

To My Mother

WHO IS IN HER EIGHTY-FIRST CREATIVE YEAR

The response to a lecture I gave several years ago on "God in Man's Creative Years," encouraged me to elaborate its points into the following chapters which I hope will be of interest to those in their middle and creative years.

What are the middle years? In writing this book I have thought of them as the years between the relative completion of our preparation for life and our retirement from living at whatever age it occurs. They are the years of reproduction and production and can be the creative years. It should be obvious to the reader that my concept of the middle years is larger and more comprehensive than is the popular concept of "middle age."

Modern novels and plays are portraying the problems of Mr. Producer and his wife and family. These storytellers challenge us by their dramatic drawing of our true portrait. In doing so, they pull off our masks which may be both therapeutic and traumatic. But what then? Do we really understand what has been revealed to us, and, if so, do we know what to do about it? After such good hard looks at ourselves many of us need help in sorting out our reactions, and in finding and using resources which will help us do something about what we now see. It is to this end that I offer the insights of the following pages.

In writing this book I have also tried to respond to the request of many readers of my earlier book, *Man's Need and God's Action,* that I elaborate further the principles found there and apply them to some of the more important areas of living. In complying with their request I found it impossible to avoid some repetition of the earlier volume but I trust that the application will make the present one new and exciting.

The mechanics of the book require a word of explanation. It opens with a chapter which reveals the thoughts of Dick Foster as he travels home from his office at the end of a day. His reverie, as it were, prepares the reader for the following chapters and raises the questions to which they are addressed. There is no attempt, however, to match exactly his questions to the thoughts of the book.

For whatever is of value in the following pages, I am indebted to the people to whom I have listened and to whom I have ministered in my capacities as priest, pastor, teacher, and counselor. These are the people who, though not named in history's record, bear the burdens of the world's life and work with courage and often without encouragement.

In particular, I wish to thank the following for their patient reading of the manuscript, in part or in full and for their helpful suggestions: Mrs. John Musser, Mrs. David Tappan, Mrs. Vernon E. Olson, Mr. Bradford Wiley, Mr. Robert Grindley, the Rev. Barton M. Lloyd, and my wife. They have contributed largely to whatever merit the following pages may have and bear no responsibility for its faults.

R. L. H.

CONTENTS

Preface vii

CHAPTER

1 INTRODUCTION: SOME QUESTIONS 1

2 THE POWER OF THE PERSONAL 19

3 THE SECRET OF OUR CREATIVITY 41

4 WHAT LOVE CAN DO 63

5 THE ROLE OF SEX IN LOVE 87

6 FIVE WAYS TO CREATIVE MARRIAGE 109

7 FOR PARENTS OF ADOLESCENTS 131

8 YOUR WORK AND YOU 165

9 FROM SECURITY TO MATURITY 189

10 A FAITH FOR THE MIDDLE YEARS 211

Suggested Readings 231

Index 237

Some Questions

1

TIME: A hot, sultry, summer afternoon.

DICK FOSTER—uneasy husband, confused father, moderately succesful businessman—is leaving his office for home.

Here I go again into the heat—everybody rushing to get home. And tomorrow I'll leave the "heat" at home and come back through these same revolving doors into this place—The Air-conditioned, Insulated Palace of Business.

Damn this heat! Walk or taxi to the station? Might as well walk—and keep to the shady side. Think I'd want some heat after that chilly business today. That was a cold session! The Boss has us all scared. Wish he'd make up his mind! Sometimes he seems to expect us to take the initiative—talks about American business based on individual enterprise, and that we all have to show what we can do. But then there's the teamwork speech: we've all got to submerge ourselves in the common enterprise. I sure stuck my neck out—suggesting we were spending too much time in meetings, that we could decide and plan better if we worked separately at our own jobs. And did I get a sermon on that one! Never heard him sound so pious. Funny, that bit about *acceptance*—we've got to accept each other no matter what. Sounded as if he was trying out a new word he had just heard. *I* sure didn't feel any acceptance! He sounded like church: long on preaching but short on practice.

I wonder if there's acceptance anywhere. Somebody's always pushing you into a mold—you don't dare be different. Well, not *too* different anyway. Look at those guys around the table this afternoon. Jack, Steve, Tom and the rest. Every one of them has ability, real ability; but not one of them has the guts to use it. Each one of us was looking at the other for the least sign of stepping out ahead. We've cooperated to the point of sterility. The only one of the bunch who dared show he agreed with me was Bob Howard—winked at me on the sly. Wonder what he was trying to prove. But, damn his eyes, he played it safe like the rest of us!

That's what Julie's always yattering at me: keep your ideas to yourself; play it safe. Always trying to save the world, and what thanks do you get for it! O hell, what's the use of ideas if you can't express them? I can't blame her, though. She's worried about the mortgage and doctors' bills and the kid's education and keeping in with the crowd. The bunch was talking about this the other night: we're concerned with our security. And it's making us all cowards. I'm afraid to be myself because I'd be different, and everyone says that if you're different you'll be lonely. Didn't somebody say that if you want to belong, you have to give up your integrity?

Why do we have to be all alike? Why do we have to junk ourselves? O yes! the group—the group is a monster that eats a man up. That's what our office staff is, a monster that says: If you want to be a part of me, you'll have to be a mouse, and don't criticize me! I wonder what would happen if I stood up for what I believed and took the consequences. I'd probably get the axe—but maybe I'd get my self-respect back again. Maybe Julie'd respect me again. Who knows, I might get a better job! It'd take guts to do that. After all, I'm 45 and am getting pushed already. Dear

God, it's hard to decide whether to play it safe or to stick
your neck out!

[*At the station*]

Judas! Look at the mob here. It's a little cooler here anyway. I wonder if any of these people . . . Look at that guy
there—looks pleased with himself—no problems. Maybe he
made his peace with the Organization—wonder what it cost
him. Wonder how his wife looks, and if she still loves him—
or did he have to sacrifice her to make things fit. Hope not.
He may be as sound as he looks. Better buy a paper and
stop this thinking. That meeting today has got me down.

[*On the train*]

Here's a seat by the window—shady side, too, thank
heavens. Let's see who did what in the paper. "Public
Enemy gets long term." I suppose the poor bird is a public
enemy. But he's not the worst one—he committed a spec-
tacular crime—but he's too obvious . . . We know who he
is and what he's doing. Feds on his trail day and night—
we've got some protection against his kind. But look at
the Boss. Never thought of it before, but he's a public
enemy, too. Measures everything in terms of his success.
Nothing means anything to him if it isn't hooked up with
his personal part in the business. He's an enemy because he
uses people in such a slick way that they admire him as a
symbol. Sort of a hidden persuader. And we don't know
that we are his victims! He's the prize manipulator.

So are some women—the one who manipulates her kids
and her husband into doing what *she* wants. In the end this
makes "things" out of them, and then she bellyaches because nobody loves her and look how I slave for all of you—
she's an enemy, too.

Worse than that—and this is me—the guy who won't

stand up and be counted, who's willing to go through life voiceless and without a face, who's always trying to figure out what answer he's expected to give. Whether it's "yes" or "no," he's the yesman. Do I sound bitter! But I'm not, really. Just trying to get things straight. Better stop this before I get home. Julie doesn't like me to carry on like this. And I suppose she's right—she's always tired—and it's no good for me to add to her problems by taking things apart. That's probably why she likes Dr. Powers' sermons, says they make her feel secure again. He's another kind of public enemy—he's always oversimplifying issues and making God seem feebleminded. He talks about love as if there wasn't any hate. His name ought to be "Dr. Miltown," the Tranquilizer. I wonder if he really believes in God? If he did, he might have the courage to face what's going on in the world and try to throw some light on it. . . . Come to think of it, we've got to go to a meeting at the church tonight. Money for more buildings. Our church costs us a lot of money and time. Julie says that if you don't put a lot in, you don't get much out. Does she give for the sake of giving or getting? Wonder what would happen if I raised the question at tonight's meeting: Why should we raise more money for another building? I wish I had the guts to ask, "What are we doing with what we've got? What's the purpose of the Church?" I can't do it; it would raise too much of a stink. I keep thinking of things and asking questions that might be a help, but I won't say them out loud so people can hear them! Time was, though, when I would have.

Questions disturb people, but who wants to be disturbed? Anyhow, we're more interested in answers than questions today. But, can answers without questions be answers? The answers we get today come from machines. They're responses, not to questions, but to an electronic pattern.

Here I am, sounding bitter again. It isn't that I've given up hope. It's just that sometimes life gets me down. I almost wish I were an Eskimo. That book I was reading the other evening said that they made a good adjustment to their environment. Why can't we make a more adequate adjustment to ours? Most folks I know don't seem convincingly happy. We're restless—seeking something—I wonder what? Whatever it is, we haven't found it, or we'd be more content. Many of our friends seem anxious about their security, but security is such a dull goal. Maybe we want solutions to our problems. This would be endless! There is no end to problems, and there probably aren't solutions to them anyhow. But I sure wish there was something to help you live with them. That's what people are looking for. That's what I'm looking for—something to live with, something that makes sense out of what happens, something that'll help me work with what I've got, something that will help me live my life. If I had *that*—whatever it is—I wouldn't be afraid to ask my questions, and I wouldn't be afraid of the answers. In fact, I don't think I would be afraid, period. I'd be able to live my life!

First stop already. Guess I must have been dozing. There goes the tired businessman. What kind of a wife has he—and kids? There they are—nice-looking family. Kids seem glad to see him and he certainly is crazy about them. Look at the hug he gives the little boy. Wife seems to take it in her stride—all he gets from her is a peck on the cheek. She's got it, too! Isn't any wife glad to see her husband? Yes, this one climbing out of the stationwagon—look at that! Acts as if she hadn't seen him since Christmas, instead of at the 8:17 this morning. Looks about my age, too—what've they got that we haven't? They're important to each other. Love's a funny thing—so easy to turn it into hate or indifference. Is that what Julie and I are looking for—an importance that won't let love turn sour?

I wish Julie and I could find it, whatever it is. I think we still love each other, but I'm afraid we don't get the idea across to each other. We don't have any time for each other any more. Living stands between us, and we can't seem to get around it to find each other. We rarely make love any more. It's always "too" something: it's too late, too early, too tired, too busy, or it's too hot or too cold. And when we do try to love each other, it doesn't come off the way it used to. Wonder if Julie's going through "change of life." I asked her once, and she seemed annoyed with me for asking her about it. I remember the time when I complained about our not loving each other more often, and she said, "Sex is all right when you're young, but as you get older, you outgrow it." Maybe *she* has, but I haven't. I want to love her as much as ever. I'm sure she wants my love, but she doesn't seem to want me to love her. If the Lord made women, he sure should've included a book of instructions with each one. Women don't seem to be as mixed up about men. Julie says she can read men like a book. If she can, she's sure dumb not to pay attention to what she reads.

I don't think that she can give herself anymore, and she's afraid of being possessed. I guess a woman gets so consumed by her children, husband, and everyone else that she has to make herself unpalatable in order to keep herself. This is what everyone is talking about—"the problem of modern women." It's not the problem of *modern* women so much as it is the *ancient* problem of women.

Oh, hell! It's so damn complicated. Sex used to be a part of our lives. Now it's incomplete and infrequent. It used to bind us together. Now it stands between us, divides us, makes us enemies. Each of us needs the other, two halves of a whole. Wonder how we ever got to the point where we have to justify sex. I'm tired of being rational and moral and spiritual. As if I weren't physical too! Look at the ads in this car! Sex appeal is sales appeal. Consumers are seduced by some part of a woman's body. The physical is exploited for commerce, but it's not really accepted as a basis for living. There's that priest over there. Wonder what he does about all this? If God's against sex, why'd He make it?

I'll bet sex is a part of Bernard and Linda's trouble. Julie and I were never able to help Bernard in this area when he was growing up. Linda's mother was mixed up in some scandal or other and Linda has never been able to talk about it much. Bernard seemed like a lonely kid. He didn't want to be cuddled, and he was never affectionate. Julie used to worry about this. I guess it was hard on her. Now with little Jane, it was different. She was eager and affectionate. It's sure hard to understand why she had that crack-up. Right before she was going to marry Ed, too. I sure feel sorry for that guy! Those kids had a tough break.

It's hard to think straight about my family, we seem so messed up. Wonder if others are like us?

I start to think about Bernard and Linda, and then I get to thinking about Jane and Ed, and that starts me off on Julie and me.

Where was I? Oh, yes, about Bernard and Linda. It was sure funny how Linda drew Bernard out. She seemed to release something in him. It must have been in him all the time. He became gay and enthusiastic. She seemed to call out all the love that he had never been able to express before. But she didn't like it. I can hear her now as she protested, "Don't paw, Bernard." I wanted to say something to them, but I didn't know how. Now, after just two years of marriage, Linda has become brittle and critical, and Bernard has become quieter, almost sullen. I had hoped that Dr. Powers would say something to them when they were married. When I asked Bernard about it, he said they only discussed the wedding service. I wonder what the point is of blessing something that is set up in such a way that it's going to fail—the blessing doesn't seem to change anything.

I was glad Bernard came to me the other day to talk about what they might do. I hope he can get Linda to go to see the family service counselor. Maybe Julie and I ought to go, too. I wonder if we're too old to be helped?

"Hello, Dick. How nice to see you!"

"Why, hello Dr. Powers, what are you doing here?"

"Just coming back from a meeting in the city, and I've been working my way through the train visiting with some of the men in the parish. Now there's time for a visit with you."

"Fine. Sit down, Dr. Powers. I was just thinking about you a little while ago."

"I hope your thoughts weren't too hard on me."

"No, I guess not. I was thinking about Bernard and Linda and about your having married them."

"They're a great couple. They'll make out all right. They're young and they have their whole life before them. By the way, how is Jane? She's really had a hard time. I must get around and see her sometime. Strange that she should change the way she did. Such an attractive child and so full of energy and love of life. When do you expect her to be released from the hospital?"

I can't talk about this with *him*. I want to but he's so darned casual. I'd have to go into Julie's and my whole life —the doctor says that this is all part of her trouble. I've got to get straight on what's going on inside of me before I can talk about Jane—or talk *to* her, for that matter. I can't say right out that Jane's trouble began way back in my relationship to Julie. Powers wouldn't know what I was talking about—and, O God, I don't either!

"The Doctor thinks she might begin to come home sometime next month."

"It's amazing what science can do for mental illness these days. It seems as if science has acquired the power to heal that religion used to have."

"Yes, I suppose that's true, but in this case, it wasn't science that healed so much as something else. By the way, do you know Mr. Duncan?"

"Do you mean that artist who is giving the popular lectures on the healing power of art? He talks about art as if it were a way of redemption."

"Yes, he's the one. I had wondered about him, too. But, he's done a lot for Jane. In fact, when Mr. Duncan came on the scene, the doctors had told us that Jane might never recover. Somehow he was able to bring her back to sanity. The head of the hospital has arranged a conference for Julie and me with him. I am wondering what he'll have to say. I'm told that he used some clay to attract her attention. You see, she wouldn't pay attention to anyone—just sat there like a dead person."

"Sounds silly to me. It's not clay but faith that heals people. Well, I must be on my way. I see Dick Andrews ahead. I must talk to him about our next financial canvas. Glad things are going so well with you. Take care of yourself."

He seems glad to get away. I never feel that he really sees or hears me. Bet he's afraid of people and of what's going on inside them. I wonder what he would have done had I told him all that I had been thinking this afternoon? Anything personal seems to make him uncomfortable. He uses religion to keep people and their troubles at a distance. Poor guy, he must be caught in the big squeeze between his own needs and the needs of his people. This must be the reason why his sermons present life in such a tidy fashion. He refers to life as a "pilgrimage." The term is too dressed up to be a good description of *my* life. When I was starting out, I thought it would be like that—that I'd be clear-eyed and brave, steadily moving toward my goal! Now, here I am in middle age, and still not sure what my goals are, and I certainly don't have any great sense of achievement.

Middle age! I guess that's the trouble. Maybe middle age is a time of crisis, just like adolescence. That's probably where the trouble began. What was that article I read the other day? Something about the adolescent being the father of the middle-ager! The author said that adolescent enthusiasms and expectations are not equal to the demands of adult life. When they fail us, their place is taken by middle-age disillusionment and slump. That was a good article.

Maybe the reason things don't seem to go right is because I'm still measuring myself and others by the standards of youth. And so is most everybody else. We're looking for the wrong things and can't appreciate what we've got. I guess middle age is bound to be disappointing if you measure it with the yardstick of youth! Maybe, if we could arrive at middle years with expectations to fit our age, we could look back on our youth as the beginning rather than the best time of our life. Well, I'll be damned, I never thought of that before!

I was going into politics. How sure I was that I would serve my country and fellow man! I studied history and political science, I held on to my dream. I knew about corruption in politics, but I was not prepared for the experience of it! I hadn't been prepared to accept it as a part of things or taught how to deal with it. I must have been pretty naive. Anyhow, I couldn't play ball. Regretted it ever since. Wonder why youngsters can't be prepared for life in other than naive or cynical ways? What good are ideals if they keep you from getting involved in the mess? Something was wrong with my education, and, from what I hear, the same thing is wrong now. I thought the author of that article hit the nail on the head when he described youth as a time when the possibilities of life are viewed without the restraints of responsibilities; that middle age is a time when responsibility is viewed with diminished hope of possibilities; and that the two ages ought to be crossed so that those who carry the responsibilities may do so with hope, and those who hope may be prepared for responsibility. That ought to be the job of education.

Yeah, our problem is the problem of middle age *versus* youth. Look at that ad for Rejuvenal. "Are you tired? Discouraged? Lost your enthusiasm? Take Rejuvenal! It will restore your youth and pep!"

Our crowd sure fits the description. We men are an ulcerous, tension-ridden, sex-obsessed, money-mad bunch who are too busy and too tired to enjoy life. And our women match us with their worry about diets and double-chins, with the problems of modern women and modern children. Both of us are lonely and scared. We're lonely because we've lost our own youth with the hopes that we had, and we're scared because of the oncoming youth that even now is pushing us aside. I guess we're afraid life is over for us. And we need more than Rejuvenal!

And we're probably breeding another generation like us, unless they are so inoculated by what happened to us that they will escape the worst ravages of life.

Julie and I tried to help Bernard and Jane. I wonder why we weren't much help? I guess there's a big gap between wanting to do something and doing it. Bernard isn't a happy person and Jane is just coming out of her breakdown. Only

Edie seems all right. But she's only twelve. I'm afraid her test is ahead of her. But it does seem as if we are more relaxed with her. Maybe you have to raise a couple of kids before you learn how. Who was it that said, "We ought to have a child, practice on him, and then throw him away and start having our family?" I guess we were too anxious with our older kids. We read too many books—were too self-conscious. I know I was always thinking: "How am I doing?" I'll bet this was a barrier between us. With Edie, it's different. To hell with the books! And we get along all right; that is, so far. Something gets into kids in their adolescence that makes them harder to understand and to handle.

Bernard was defiant, as if he were trying to prove something—a chip on his shoulder—daring me to knock it off. I couldn't make up my mind whether he was making a bid for more discipline or whether I wasn't giving him enough freedom. And this didn't help him, I guess. I failed him as a father without knowing why. He had a way of making me awfully angry. It's funny how the feeling of helplessness makes you angry. Then I'd feel guilty about my resentment of him. We lost touch with each other during his teens. Something came between us. I've often wished we could get it out and talk about it. Now, lately, things seem a little better, and I'm glad he came to me the other day. Maybe we can work things out now. I sure hope he and Linda get some help!

With Jane it was different. She was such an eager little thing, and she obviously wanted to please everybody, especially her mother. They were very close when she was little. When she reached her teens, the strains began. Yet after she had been defiant about something, she couldn't do enough to show how sorry she was. She could never stand quarrels. Sometimes they really made her sick. She was always a peacemaker. And she worked awfully hard for approval. She was almost too cooperative. Sometimes Julie worried about Jane because she was too good. She felt Jane did not look out for her own interests enough. I couldn't see anything wrong with her, but something must have been. We gave her everything, including love. According to the theory, that's the answer . . . I suppose it's like a lot of other theories, it's all right until you try to put it to work.

Well, there's the red barn—time to get off. Sure hope it's cooler. Wonder if there will be time for a swim? Wish Jane were home; she'd love to go with me. I hate to think of her locked up in that hospital. She was such a gay, wild little thing, in spite of all her sober concerns. Maybe Julie will go with me. Well, here we are . . .

[*The walk home*]

Still hot! Too hot to walk—but doctor's orders—good for my pot and other ailments. Have to keep the machinery going. The old body isn't as good as it used to be. Doc says that I'm at the age when I *must* live right. He means: go easy on the drinks, late nights, too vigorous exercise. He's right, sure! But that's not what gets me down. It's the tension, the competition with the other guy, like Jim Crowthers, who's crowding up from the bottom. I'm in a big squeeze. The other fellows are in it, too, but we don't let on to each other that we are. It's sure lonely. If misery loves company, wonder why we don't admit it—it might relax things a bit. If I'm lucky, I'll enjoy the tidy finish of a heart attack. Otherwise, I'll enjoy the more moderate blessing of uselessness and senility under the benefits of social security.

I'll soon be home. What a strange word—*home*. Is it the word, or is it me that makes it strange? Julie doesn't look for me any more. I guess she no longer expects me. Sometimes when I arrive, I feel as if I weren't there. She'll absent-mindedly say, "Oh, hello." It's as if I appear to say "hello" and then reappear momentarily tomorrow morning to say "good-bye." I feel like an image that has become unhooked from the person to whom it belongs. I wish I could step up on the porch, say, "Julie!"—have her look at me and *see* me; and that in speaking her name, I could really see her again!

I don't really feel that low about things, or do I? If I do, I probably should not admit it, even to myself. Have to keep up appearances. Wonder what would happen if everyone admitted how they felt about the lives they were living. I'll bet the trains and elevators would stop running, business would collapse, preachers would drop dead in their pulpits, and criminals would become saints. If true, it's a miracle that things go on. The courage of survival! For what? God, I'm tired!

So's Julie. I can hear her now. But things haven't been easy for her, either. There's a lot in her that's been stifled. Wish I could help, but I guess I'm the cause of a lot of her trouble. I wish we didn't have to go to that meeting tonight. That's right, I'd forgotten; I guess there won't be time for a swim. There's no end. Every meeting I attend makes necessary at least one or two more. Who the hell said, "Real life is meeting"? I'd say that real life would be not meeting!

There's Bert. What a beautiful yard he has! He's always working in it. His sure shows up the rest of our places. Says it's the only thing that keeps him going, that he'd go nuts without it. Well, at least he can see some results for his labors. Maybe he's right. He always used to be in a stew about something. Now he doesn't seem to care. He's in a squeeze in his company and may be included out already. And at his age that's serious. But he seems to have accepted the fact that the new adventures are over—and he goes on planting those damned dahlias! Wish I could take it like that. Wonder what would happen if I could make some of my decisions over again—would I be the same person— wonder if I'd know what to do?

That story I read the other day, funny I should think of it now. About the old man who was lost in a forest and met a ranger, who asked him, "Who are you, and where are you going?" The old man was so impressed with the ranger's questions that after he found his way out of the forest, he hired the man and made him wake him each morning, asking, "Who are you? Where are you going?" Who am I? Where am I going? That's what it all boils down to, I guess. But how am I going to find the answer? I wish I didn't have to do this all alone.

There's my house, and there's Edie waiting for someone —could it be for me? She used to watch for me. Then, she'd run and throw her arms about me, and all in one breath tell me her whole day. Now she's becoming a young lady and learning adult ways, which means she hides herself from others. Why is that the adult way? Why do we pretend an independence and an indifference to others that we do not feel?

Well, there's Julie on the porch.

"Hi, Julie. Isn't it hot?"

"Oh, hello."

CHAPTER 2

The Power of the Personal

"I can't talk about this with him. I'd have to go into Julie's and my whole life—the doctor says that this is part of Jane's trouble. I've got to get straight on what's going on inside of me before I can talk about Jane—or talk to her, for that matter. . .

"Julie and I tried to help Bernard and Linda. I wonder why we weren't much help? I guess there's a big gap between wanting to do something and doing it. Only Edie seems all right. But she's only twelve. I'm afraid her test is ahead of her. . .

"I thought the author of that same article hit the nail on the head when he described youth as a time when the possibilities of life are viewed without the restraints of responsibilities; that middle age is a time when responsibility is viewed with diminished hope of possibilities; and that the two ages ought to be crossed so that those who carry the responsibilities may do so with hope, and those who hope may be prepared for responsibility . . ."

—Dick Foster

2 We are all looking for a way of becoming persons, a way of finding ourselves and of achieving a sense of self that is unpretentious and authentic. We are looking for a power of being that is equal to all the questions, demands, relationships, and responsibilities of life. But what is the nature of this power? Where shall we find it?

We seek this power in various places. Some of us have sought it in study courses on personality—but it was not to be found there. Instead, we found merely descriptions of personality that did not tell us how to find the power to be a person. Others of us put faith in formulas on how to influence people, but soon discovered that power over people is not the power of the personal for which we were seeking.

i

The power of the personal is the power to hear and to help one another, and, incidentally, to be heard and helped ourselves; the power to live together with mutual helpfulness and creativeness. The power of the personal may not seem like power because it does not reveal itself in the same way aggressive power does. And because it does not make a show of itself, we must not think it weak and martyr-like. I remember being surprised by the power of the personal in a teacher who even described herself as timid, and whom I thought was so timid and meek as to be ineffective. She had been assigned to a school with a number of difficult children. On the very first day she had trouble with a sullen, rebellious fourteen-year-old named Joe, who recognized her as an ideal person to bully. For several weeks she tried to gain control of him and of the class. But instead, she became more frightened and insecure, and the class more difficult since it followed Joe's lead in everything he did to upset her. Finally, one afternoon, in desperation and without knowing what would happen, she kept him after school and asked him why he was picking on her.

For a moment he looked sullenly at her and then replied, "Because you're such a sucker for it."

"I know I am," she sighed. "I've always been afraid of people like you, and yet I'd like to be able to help you. Isn't there some other reason why you're always fighting and picking on people who can't take care of themselves? Don't you want anyone to love you or help you?"

Much to her amazement, the fourteen-year-old bully broke down, cried, and told her the story of the misery, loneliness, and hostility that lay hidden behind his rebelliousness. Her honesty as a person called forth the truth from this confused and resentful boy; it helped free him of his hostility so that he could begin to find constructive ways of working out his problems. Having experienced the power of the personal from one who as a person did not seem to have much power, he was set on the way, through her, to becoming a person. On the other hand, her strength rested, to no small degree, in her ability to be honest about her timidity. And that honesty reached him so that he knew she accepted him, his anxiety about himself, and his hostility toward her. In other words, her power to accept herself became her power to accept him, and this made it possible for him in turn to accept himself. This is what we mean by the power of the personal: *The power to help one another to become and remain persons.*

Evidence, on the one hand, of our need of the personal and, on the other hand, of our ignorance of its power and importance is seen in the following story.

In his youth, Brooks Adams made this entry in his diary: "Went fishing with my father—the most glorious day of my life." And so great was the influence of this one day's personal experience with his father that for thirty years thereafter he made repeated references in his diary to the glowing memory of that day.

The rest of the story has a frightening aspect to it. Strangely enough, Brooks' father, Charles Francis Adams, onetime ambassador to Great Britain, made a different comment, in his diary about the same day and incident: "Went fishing with my son. A day wasted."[1]

Here we have the thrilled response of a boy to what seemed to him to be the personal interest and companionship of someone very important to him. At the same time we have the blindness of that same adult to the significance of what he was doing in terms of the power of the personal. Here is illustrated both our need of the personal and our ignorance of its power and importance.

Our own age is marked by the same conflict and confusion about the personal that we find in the Adams diaries. On the one hand, we are rediscovering the power of the personal through social and psychological research; and on the other, we are a part of a social order that often bypasses persons in order to use them. Through the exercise of the power of the personal, men and women all over the world are being restored to life and hope; but because of the exploitation of people by organizations, the life of the personal is impaired if not destroyed. We grow more proficient in the making and selling of our products, but we are not as successful in living with our neighbors, local or international. Indeed, the world of the personal baffles and threatens us. And since the world of the technical is easier to live in and gives us what sense of accomplishment we have, it has gradually become the master, and the personal

[1] Dr. Joseph Rayback, State College, Pennsylvania, is the source of my information about this incident.

its slave. This enslavement of the personal by the technical effects human life in various ways, one very noticeable effect being the sense of anxiety it arouses in us.

When the social order exploits the personal, anxiety is increased. We feel more vulnerable than ever. We feel impelled to find ways of reassuring ourselves that we *are* and that we are important. We may do this by competing with one another for recognition, or we may accumulate the things of this world in order to tell the world and ourselves that our life has meaning. Either by the love of things or by treating people as things, we try to justify our existence and authenticate ourselves. And this way of living reveals how pervasive and deep is our sense of anxiety.

Dick Foster voiced this anxiety several times. He and the rest of us are anxious because of the shortness of our lives, the menacing approach of death, and the sense of guilt that gnaws at our moral vitals. So powerful is this sense of anxiety that we spend both considerable money and time in our attempt to allay it. This anxiety is not something that a doctor can heal because it comes with the man; it is built into him and he cannot exist without it. It is deeper than the fear of the atom bomb or anything else identifiable that can be fought or endured. Anxiety, in contrast to fear, is hard to deal with because it has no identifiable object or source; it lurks vaguely and menacingly in the background of consciousness. We usually know why we are afraid, but anxiety comes and goes without passport or explanation, an ominous threat to our being.

We began this chapter with the question: Where shall we find the power to become persons? how can we find the power of being whereby we can be ourselves, and, at the same time, freely and meaningfully participate in the life of others? Maybe were we to find this balance, we would have the answer to our anxieties.

No one today who understands people at all can possibly question the need for an answer to anxieties. The experience of Dick Foster on coming to his present job when he was forty years old, illustrates for us this need for an answer. On the eve of assuming his new responsibilities, he became anxious and fearful that he might not measure up to them. The story he told revealed that through the years he had carried with him feelings of personal insecurity in the form of a fear that he would not come up to the expectations of others. To make matters worse, he was drivingly ambitious and held himself to perfectionistic standards of performance. He admitted that this contributed considerably to his anxiety. He drove himself and others unmercifully in his strenuous struggle for recognition. Recognition, however, failed to reassure him, so he strove all the more for it in the hope that eventually he would be able to respect himself as a person. The aggressiveness by which he tried to win this needed recognition did not endear him to his associates. His consequent sense of aloneness added to his anxiety.

One reason for this difficulty of Dick's was that when he thought about his job, he pictured himself as the only person on it who was active and responsible. He it was who had to think up all the questions and answers; only he could influence the issues and make the decisions. He was unable to picture as vividly the possible thought and action in the situation of the other people around him; and, therefore, he was unable to have confidence in any contribution they might make. Feeling himself isolated, he was always afraid that, by himself, he would not be able to think of all the things necessary to bring a project to a successful conclusion.

Another cause of Dick's loneliness and anxiety was the fierce competition in which he found himself, as a member of a modern business organization, to advance, or even to maintain, himself on his job. The need to compete under-cuts the support that, otherwise, might have come from men who were members of the same organization. The power of competition to prevent people from genuinely cooperating with one another often short-circuits the power of the personal.

Here we have a capable producer, a person of responsi-bility whose way of life finally caught up with him and induced a crisis in which he was forced to confront himself and his relation to others. And what was the meaning of his situation? He had an image of himself as a confident, masterful, producing person. He had tried to match the image by striving to be this kind of person. He had failed because he could not accept that part of himself which did not fit the image. His efforts to prove himself alienated him from his fellows. He was alone and, therefore, without any-one to whom he could turn for help in his time of need.

In light of this interpretation, we are now ready to draw an important conclusion about the kind of power we must have to be ourselves and to be participants in life. *We need that power that is able to help us to accept the unacceptable in ourselves.* The unacceptable is the source of the anxiety that destroys us. Dick, the would-be executive, could not tolerate Dick the man who tires, and is lonely and fallible. It was this in himself from which he sought to hide. The unacceptable in ourselves, as in Dick, causes us to undertake the strenuous and futile task of self-justification.

ii

Who can save us from that vain process? To answer this question we must first explore the process by which we become a person. The story of Joe and his teacher at a decisive moment in that process will serve to illustrate what we mean. His efforts to affirm himself as a person led him to be a bully and to pick on people who, outwardly, were like his hidden and unacceptable self. His belligerence was a sign of his anxiety about himself and of how he thought he "rated" with others. His need for love was so great and painful that he covered it up. Since he couldn't accept this need as a part of himself, he was forced to prove to himself and others that he was strong and self-sufficient. Beneath a rough and bullying exterior throbbed the terrible suffering of a lonely boy. But his teacher saw beneath the surface and accepted *for him* the unacceptable part of him, and loved him. This helped him to give up his false role and to be himself.

As children, we all depended upon our parents and teachers so to live for us that we could live increasingly for ourselves and for others. By their acceptance of us, we were better able to accept ourselves. Their love for us revealed that we were lovable even when we were unlovable, so that we learned to love ourselves and could begin to grow in the power to love others. The power-of-being in them awakened and nurtured the power-of-being in us. Our self-hood gradually emerged in response to their care of us as persons. We were dependent upon them for awakening in us the awareness of ourselves as persons and, within that relationship, for allowing us the freedom to affirm ourselves as persons. But the time came when it was necessary for us to withdraw from this first form of the filial relationship because it had outlived its usefulness.

This moment of withdrawal from relationship for the sake of self-awareness is a crucial moment in the history of the individual. It is the moment that deeply influences what power of being he will have. It is also a moment of great confusion for everyone—for the individual, for his parents, and for all who have the care of him. It is a stage of development which we do not understand as well as we should. For example, we are firm in our belief about the role of relationship in the emergence of persons: that only as we live with others do we become persons and that the first important community is the family. Of this we are sure. But during adolescence something happens which, at first glance, seems to contradict this principle of persons appearing out of relation.

All young people come to a time in their lives when they are possessed by a need to withdraw from the close, intimate, and confidential relationship they had as children. They need to be alone. The withdrawal is both physical and psychological. Their thoughts are not as open as they used to be, but are more locked up in them. They need to repudiate the parental standards, tastes, ideas, faiths, and ways of doing. They rebel against parental supervision and interference. They become secretive and morose. They seem preoccupied and thoughtful. These, and all the other characteristics that we might name, are signs that the youngster is trying to disentangle that which is himself from all that is not himself. To accomplish this he must go apart for a while, withdraw into himself. He must isolate himself momentarily in order to examine the results of having lived in relationship.

Not only young people, but great leaders in times of crisis have always had to do this. Even our Lord, nurtured by Mary and Joseph, was driven after His baptism into the wilderness to be alone for forty days while He struggled for an awareness of who He was. He emerged out of this time of isolation with a new concept of Himself and His mission. So radical was the change that even those who were closest to Him and to the tradition out of which He came had difficulty understanding and accepting Him and His life. So, likewise, each of us in his respective way is driven into a "wilderness" of aloneness from which each hopes to emerge with a power to be himself, and, as such, to be in relation.

Only in radical loneliness do we find ourselves. But the loneliness has to be prepared for by nurturing relationships. Without them we could not face the risks of withdrawal, of going apart from those who love us and whom we love, but from whom we must be free.

Equally important, however, is the role of the family or the community during this time of withdrawal and testing. Its attitude and action during this period of self-discovery must be supportive or the youngster will fail to accomplish his purpose.

The tensions of youth's withdrawal test the community severely, because the search for self on the part of the adolescent often appears to the community as a repudiation of all that it holds dear. Furthermore, it all too often looks as if the family had failed. Actually, however, this repudiation is often a sign of success. The family needs insight and courage to accept itself, including its anxieties, in order that it may be free to accept the person who is disturbing the relationship. Such acceptance will enable him to sort out his thoughts and feelings, his faiths and loyalties, his standards and goals, and emerge from the testing time with some awareness of who he is, and with a more mature capacity for the old, as well as the new, relationships.

An incident that illustrates the kind of acceptance which this situation demands occurred years earlier between Dick Foster and his son, Bernard. Bernard wanted to break away from the family and go off on his own for the summer, but both his father and mother were afraid to let him go. One evening, while Dick was reading the evening paper, Bernard tackled him again on the subject.

"I don't want to go on the same old trip to the mountains with you and the family. . . . Gosh, I'm not a baby any more. I would like to try running my own life for a change. . . . Last summer Nick's dad gave him fifty bucks and an old jalopy and let him just take off. . . . He worked his way out to the coast, working on farms, and had swell times with all kinds of people. It was hard work but he had a keen time. But you and Mom would never let me do that. You'll make me go along to the mountains with all your stupid friends and their stupid children. I hate it!"

Having stated his case, Bernard eyed his father with defiance and anxiety. Dick looked at his son and remembered his own youth with the result that this was one of the times when he acted with understanding and acceptance.

"O.K., Bernard. I'll see what I can do. Your mother's not going to like it, but I'll give you your chance to go it yourself. Since you asked for it, you're on your own."

Bernard looked at his father with amazement, but manfully he walked out of the room, and Dick resumed his reading. In a few moments, however, the boy returned,

"Dad," he said, "I'd like to ask you something. You'd . . . you'd . . . if I got stuck, you'd help me out, wouldn't you?" he ended with a rush.

"Sure," replied Dick. "Of course, I would."

This little incident beautifully sums up the adolescent's predicament, the parent's opportunity, and the kind of relationship out of which is born creative, affirmative selfhood.

On that occasion Dick had been able to provide the acceptance that would help his son break free of the old dependence and begin to find himself as an independent person, capable of a new and much to be desired man-to-man relationship with his father. Had he been annoyed by Bernard's defiance and unable to accept him for what he had to do as a person, the boy would have been caught in a conflict between rejection by his father and the inner need to break away from the childhood pattern. Indeed, in his state of rejection, he would have resented his father and felt guilty about his need and desire to become himself.

iii

Under circumstances of rejection the work of youth cannot be accomplished. *Escape from youth is possible only when the work of youth is done.* The meaning of this truth for the middle years of our lives is not as clear as it needs to be.

The truth begins to be apparent, however, when we realize the work that youth has to accomplish. *First, as we have already noted, he has to make the transition from childhood to adulthood, to change from a "taking in" individual to a "giving out" person.* He has to become himself and must cease to be known as the child of his parent.

Second, to be oneself means to be "called out" from a dependence on others and "called to" a responsibility for others. This is what we mean by vocation—"to be called." Everyone has a vocation, everyone is called, but not everyone knows it or knows what the call is. If we do not know that we are called, we cannot very well respond, which means that we cannot complete the work of youth, and, therefore, we are not ready and equal to the responsibilities and relationships of the middle years.

All too often a call is thought about in terms of a special mission and task. The simplest way of understanding a call is in terms of that to which we give our lives. The answer to the question "Whom or what do we serve?" tells us whose call we have heard. We may serve truth or the prejudices of some group; we may serve God and man or our own selfish aims; we may serve love or lust. But we must understand that, in serving, we are responding to a call. Of course, many of us serve masters without knowing who they are. The gift of ourselves was made without thought or decision. Youth is a time when we become aware that there is a self to be given, and a time when preparation for, and training in, commitment should be received. Commitment is indispensable for a creative adulthood, as the well-known prayer states, "O God . . . whose service is perfect freedom." An uncommitted life is a chaotic life, a slavery to everything and everybody. But in singlehearted service there is great freedom. An important work of youth, therefore, is the giving of the new found self. Here, family, church, and school have a wonderful opportunity to encourage, challenge, and guide the youth so that he may hear and respond to the highest call.

Another aspect of vocation is our work, or job. This is our most common understanding of the word "vocational guidance," "vocational aptitude," and "vocational choice." This is a limited meaning of the word. Actually our job is but one of the ways in which we can express our vocation, one way in which we can serve the ultimate value to which we have given our lives. This relation of vocation to daily work will be discussed in a later chapter.

But now we need to understand that if a young person is able to choose his job, he needs help to choose it as a way of serving his life's purpose. His vocational choice should be influenced by his life commitment. If he wants to give his life to the alleviation of human suffering, he might, for example, choose work in either the medical or the social field. On the other hand, if he is not free to choose his job and finds himself engaged in a business mainly because it is a way to earn a living, he may still conduct his business in ways that both prevent and minister to the needs of men. In other words, he may still use the job that has fallen to him as one way of living his commitment. When this work of youth is done, the person is on the way to a creative adulthood.

A third work of youth is the achievement of a capacity for sexual relationship. More is begun toward the achievement of this than is *effected* during adolescence. The achievement of sexual maturity and relationship requires a lifetime. In his earliest years man's erotic life and its emotional satisfaction center in himself. In later childhood he begins to enjoy playing and working with others, but chiefly with those of the same sex as himself. Having moved from self to others of the same sex, his interest and desires next center in others of the opposite sex. And, of course, this change in center coincides with other changes which are also taking place within the individual. Prior to adolescence, the erotic life of the individual, in the adult sense, is diffused and nonsexual; while during adolescence, it becomes specific and genital, moving in the direction of the individual's choosing and being chosen by a partner for a relation of mutual and exclusive commitment.

When the young person comes to this stage in his development, he undergoes a radical transformation in every aspect of his life. The new powers and the new kinds of relationships which are beginning to appear are both frightening and attractive. What *is* a man? What *is* a woman? What does go on between them? What does it mean? For the first time he is becoming aware of the fathomless depths of being, of meanings that carry him far beyond the limits of the world he has hitherto known. The external regulations and laws by which he was previously governed now seem to guide him from within. He begins to correct his parents by the same standards they used to train him. He has new ideals and new powers of thought and speech. He has a new passion for living which brings a new power of being. But there is also a new sense of incompleteness, and a longing for intimacy with someone who will fill the void. And, with all this, there is a new sense of anxiety. In these years the individual knows for the first time that he is death-doomed; and against this sense of doom his faith will begin its struggle—sometimes frantically, sometimes pathetically, sometimes courageously, and, sometimes, we hope, victoriously.

All this is what it means to be a person. On the one hand, there is the sense of blessing as he eagerly seeks to know, possess, and affirm himself; on the other hand, there is the mystery of being, within which he himself, as well as others, remains unknown. His faith is beset with doubt; and that which seems so surely true is threatened by the possibility of being without meaning.

Since growth through the teen-age years into adulthood involves such a tremendous transformation, it is accompanied by signs of real upheaval. Teenagers will say and do strange things, from indulging in "jive" talk and ducktail haircuts to reckless driving and occasional wanton destruction of property. Is it not clear that young people, going through these unsettling years, need an accepting and understanding community in which they may live through their renascence? This acceptance does not mean that we allow them to do as they please—to drive 90 miles per hour through town. To allow them unrestrained license to say and do all they feel would be to abandon them. They would be left on their own to find their way through the confused tangle of life with nothing to help them find a sense of direction. They would be deprived of the sense of order which a healthy discipline can offer them, and of the understanding support which they need as they live through the stormy experiences through which they must pass before they can reach the surer ground of adulthood. This calls for understanding, understanding in the sense of "standing under" them during these years, knowing that much of what is happening is a developmental necessity. But acceptance means raising questions as well as enduring patiently; it means to challenge as well as to agree; it means to make mistakes, to lose temper, even to hate, but also to acknowledge and confess, to forgive and to be forgiven. *An accepting community is a haven in which faith in one another prevails even though that faith is sorely tested.* In this kind of community, youth is able to do its work: to begin to leave the tormented, withdrawn period and to carry forward into maturity the kind of personality that brings new life to every relationship. It is by this process we become beneficiaries of the power of the personal and also instruments of that same power.

iv

It is through the power of the personal, also, that we find the answers to the questions we have been asking in this chapter. Through the power of the personal, the child is accepted, even though always imperfectly. Through the experience of being accepted, he comes to the point where he has the courage and trust to break from the relationship with parents which until now has been the chief source of life and love for him. Through the power of the personal, he is better able to accept himself and emerge from the adolescent years of searching and testing with some powers of self-affirmation and self-giving. Through the power of the personal, he is better able to accept others, and to assume the responsibilities of husband, father, and brother's keeper. Again, we see how important it is for us to have completed the work of youth in order that we may be free to live as mature and creative adults.

If we have really moved and grown into adulthood, we

no longer need to be defensive nor pretend to be what we are not. When, by the power of the personal, we have been accepted, we are more free to be ourselves and more free to be open to the selves of others. To the degree this state of being prevails, we shall need less the illusions of youth, and we shall fear less the mediocrity of middle-age. We shall move into the middle years with a renewing interest and creativity. The meaning of life will increase and deepen for us.

This does not mean that everything will be lovely. Quite the opposite may often be true. The power of the personal to accept the unacceptable in ourselves and others must embrace even its enemies—hate, envy, and fear—as a part of its life. Illustrations of this mixing of love and hate are common.

Many people have difficulty accepting hate, in any of its manifestations, as a part of love; but we find evidence of it everywhere. A mother recently told how her little girl, with arms tightly around her, sobbed out in real frustration: "I hate you, Mommy. I hate you. You won't let me stay up." And her mother comforted her by holding her and saying, "I know, darling, I know." Out of this kind of experience are deep relationships built.

The presence of hate in a relationship of love is for all of us a profound threat. Many a couple has concluded that because they resented each other, they no longer loved each other. Because love is indispensably important to them, and because hate to them means the failure and death of love, they may try to deny the existence of hate. The deception fails because they are not accepting the whole experience of love. By hiding the hostility, it is not available to love's power to redeem it. It is, therefore, free to undermine and destroy the relationship.

The act of accepting hate as a part of love is an act of love which opens us to the power of love. Here are some of the deepest works that the power of the personal has to do: accepting the unacceptable; accepting hate as a part of the love relationship. We need the power of the personal if we are to deal with the problems of personal life. But it is also true that we will not grow in the power of the personal unless we face our personal difficulties.

Many relationships are destroyed because of accumulated resentments. The husband may have said something that irritates his wife. She says nothing. She bottles up her anger which daily gets worse. But she can't talk about what really concerns her and so begins to fuss with him about little things. He retaliates and soon their love is lost in a jungle of hostilities. These are the problems of the personal that are crying out for the healing power of the personal. And what is this healing power? Judge John Warren Hill of the New York Domestic Relations Court gives us a clue when he advises: "Talk it out!" By talking out the difficulty, the couple *as persons* are available to each other. Their understanding and love are given something to work on. Thus some married couples never experience the fullest meaning of their union because they will not use the resources of love to face their real problems. Not only do they fail to gain what they might have achieved together, but they lose what they had.

Our thought thus far in this chapter is both encouraging and discouraging. Our thought may have even given us a new sense of power in the personal, a realization that the greatest thing that a human being can be and do is to be a person living in responsible relation with his neighbor. All this is good. But we are probably greatly discouraged, too. When we look at the complexity of human relationships, not only the individual face-to-face relationships but the local and world-community ones as well, we cannot help but turn away with something of despair. We know that, because we are men, mortal and selfish, we of ourselves cannot do all that needs to be done.

This sense of disparity between what we can do and what needs to be done is one of the most common causes of our middle-age compromises and of the consequent loss of initiative, enthusiasm, and belief in our creative potential. The same sense of disparity accounts for the prevalence of illness among us, distractive living, and other symptoms of our lost illusions about ourselves, about others, and about the world in which we live.

What can we put in the place of lost illusions? *First, we need to agree that it is good to lose illusions.* Home, church, and school ought to combine forces to combat the formation of illusions, and to replace them when they exist. This is all the more necessary today when every means of communication is being employed by "producers" to instill and nurture illusions in "consumers" that will cause them to buy. The new illusions are that we will be acceptable if we buy some product, use that aid to distinction, do that thing without which no man can hope to succeed. The exploitation of the universal need to be accepted produces false standards and beliefs. We must resist this effort to replace lost illusions with new ones.

Second, the only effective replacement for illusions is a faith. And this is the answer to our frustration at the disparity between our own power of the personal and our need for it. Our power of the personal is rooted in God and in His forgiveness. He alone can finally accept the unacceptable, which is described as the chief work of the personal. Without the Cross, on which God accepted all that was opposed to Him, all that would negate Him, all that was unacceptable to Him, it would be impossible for us to accept, as a part of our own lives, all that threatens our existence. Therefore, our power of the personal is rooted in the action of the Person of Christ, who so completely took upon Himself our experiences that He cried out: "My God, My God, why hast thou forsaken me?" Thus, our power of the personal is rooted in this same Person, Jesus Christ, who, having taken unto Himself all the threats of our being, was raised from the dead. The Resurrection can mean for us the ultimate and final victory of the power of the personal. Our faith in the personal is, therefore, justified.

His acceptance of the unacceptable is made available to us now by His Spirit. He calls to us in every relationship and aspect of our lives. Who can deny that His working is not to be recognized in generous impulses, in acts of kindness and consideration? And there are our responses to His calling which open us more to His activity.

Thus, we may believe that His Power of Love will be in every act of love; that His Power of Acceptance will be in every act of acceptance; and that His Power of the Personal will be in every personal encounter. If we offer ourselves to Him as His instrument, He will speak and act through us. Thus, the Church may become increasingly the community of the accepted and the accepting, the instrument of the power of the personal accepting the unacceptable.

Here is the faith for the community that must provide the accepting context for youth's search. Here is the faith for men and women, who, passing over the threshold of maturity, face relationships in which they will experience love and hate, faith and doubt, life and death. Here is the faith that will save us from having to rely upon the un-worked out illusions of youth; the faith that will save us from the necessity of despair and resignation, from everything that produces the slump of our middle years. Our faith is in Him, who is the Source of the Power of the Personal.

With this faith, we need not fear to turn to some of the problems of our middle years.

CHAPTER 3

The Secret of Our Creativity

"It's amazing what science can do for mental illness these days," continued Dr. Powers. "It seems as if science has acquired the power to heal that religion used to have."

"Yes, I suppose that's true, but in this case, it wasn't science that healed so much as something else. By the way, do you know George Duncan?" asked Dick.

"Do you mean that artist who is giving the popular lectures on the healing power of art? He talks about art as if it were a way of redemption."

"Yes, he's the one. I had wondered about him, too. But, he's done a lot for Jane. In fact, when Mr. Duncan came on the scene, the doctors had told us that Jane might never recover. Somehow he was able to bring her back to sanity. The head of the hospital has arranged a conference for Julie and me with him. I am wondering what he'll have to say. I'm told that he used some clay to attract her attention. You see, she wouldn't pay attention to anyone—just sat there like a dead person."

Dr. Powers snorted. "Sounds silly to me. It's not clay but faith that heals people. Well, I must be on my way. I see Dick Andrews ahead. I must talk to him about our next financial canvas. Glad things are going so well with you. Take care of yourself."

—Dick Foster

3 When we come to our mature years, we especially need all our creative powers because it is at this period we carry our heaviest family, civic, and job responsibilities. Unfortunately, however, by the time this period arrives, many of us have already lost our sense of creativity. We have lost confidence in ourselves, as well as the courage and freedom to "stick out" our necks—in a word, the courage to take the normal risks of creative living is gone. We find ourselves bumping along in ever deeper ruts, and the thought of tearing ourselves out of them seems more and more impossible. Even when we get a good opportunity to break our set patterns, we are afraid to take the chance, afraid to risk upsetting our creaking applecart.

We would like to find our youthful attitude again, and the confidence it gave us. But there is no going back to our youth and no Fountain of Youth in which we can dunk and renew our spirit. We cannot live our lives again, nor is there any magic by which we can be changed. The answer to middle-aged doldrums, however, is not to go back but *to move forward,* and, in so doing, to find in each moment its deeper meanings and possibilities. The joys and promise of youth may be gone, but the joys and fulfillments of the middle years are there for those who will go after them.

There are undoubtedly many reasons why we lose our enthusiasm, confidence, and creativity, but it is not the purpose of this chapter to analyze fully all that. *Instead, our purpose is to see that the way we live together influences the growth of creativity in us.* We have all seen children begin life full of fun and energy but, in a few years, become dull and indifferent. Usually the explanation for the change is that something hurtful has happened between them and some person important to them. Instead of being able to use their originality and energy for living, they have had to use it to defend and hide themselves. I have seen graduate students fail, while trying to prepare for what they hoped would be creative work, because their creativity was locked up inside their noncommittal and defensive personalities. When it was possible to get behind their defenses, they revealed that they had covered over their true selves because they had learned that it was not safe to be enthusiastic, generous, experimental, and different.

i

The story of Jane Foster, the daughter of Dick and Julie, provides a moving illustration of how people through their relations with others can both lose and find their creativity. Some aspects of the story are so unusual that the reader may be tempted to think that its meaning could not possibly apply to him. The meaning of the story, however, is applicable to every one and should be read with that expectation.

Jane had been a lovely young girl, and her parents had done their best to give her every advantage. She was most attractive and popular, and had many talents. In her twenty-first year, she fell in love with an able and handsome young man. On the eve of their marriage she collapsed and the ceremony had to be indefinitely postponed. At first, it seemed as if she were exhausted and that a good rest was all that she needed. Her condition grew worse, however. She was depressed, made several attempts to take her life, and finally had to be taken to a mental hospital. Even there, she deteriorated until she would do nothing for herself, simply sat in a corner, day after day, looking at the floor, a pathetic contrast to the bright pixie creature she used to be.

Naturally, her family and close friends were shocked at this change in her, for which there seemed to be no explanation. The doctors talked to her parents, her fiancé, and others who might throw light on her case. But her condition remained the same—inert, sullen, silent. The weeks in which she remained in this condition passed into months, and the months into a year.

Toward the end of the year, Dr. Miller, superintendent of the hospital where Jane was a patient, began sitting for his portrait. The artist, George Duncan, encouraged Dr. Miller to talk about his work. One day Dr. Miller told him about Jane's case and confessed his sense of helplessness.

"As in all such cases, the person remains inaccessible. Nothing that we say seems to reach her; and she says nothing."

"What have you done to try to bring her out of wherever she is?" asked the artist.

"Well, we've given her the usual treatments, but not even shock treatments have the expected effect on her. I've sent the chaplain in to see her, but he admits defeat. Says he can't do anything, and she doesn't seem even to hear him."

George Duncan went on painting while the doctor continued to talk about the case. Finally, he put down his brushes with a remark about the failing light, and asked if he might see Jane. They left the doctor's office and went down the long, lonely white corridors of the hospital to the room where Jane sat on the floor in the corner. The artist stood on the threshold, looking at the girl, who seemed more dead than alive—a human being whose spirit had departed, leaving only a mechanically breathing body. All signs of animation and creativity were gone, and only hopeless isolation remained. Jane was the complete embodiment of despair and defeat, a condition that on occasion we all experience partially.

The artist just stood there for a few moments, looking at the girl. Then he moved slowly toward her, at the same time drawing something from his coat pocket. Then he stooped down and held out in his hand, under her apparently unseeing eyes, a lump of clay that he gently molded with his fingers. There was no indication of response from the girl; in a few moments he rose to his feet and went out with the doctor.

"May I drop in and see Jane whenever I come to work on your portrait?" he asked. "Her condition challenges my belief in the inherent creativity of people, and I'd like to try to reach her."

Permission was readily granted, and each time Duncan finished his work on the portrait, he went back to see Jane. And each time he repeated the routine of his first visit. He stooped down, held out his hand before Jane's eyes, and slowly worked the clay with his fingers. The portrait was finished, but he still continued to come back to the hospital to visit Jane. One day she timidly reached out her hand and touched the clay. On another of his visits, she took it in her hand. Later she took the clay and closed her fingers around it; and when she opened them, she looked wonderingly at the impression she had made on the clay.

Visit followed visit, and each time there was a little more response. Then, one day, she worked the clay with both hands, slowly and hesitantly; hers was the unmistakable action of a person once again beginning to respond to the stir of life. But never, during all this, did she lift her head or look at the artist. Her appearance continued to be that of one afraid.

In all these weeks the artist had not spoken to Jane either, but had trusted only in what he could say through his presence and actions. Finally, one day when she was working the clay into rude shapes, he spoke her name softly: "Jane." Her hands paused, her head came up slowly, and with caution she looked at him, the first person she had looked at for months. No one can really know what happened between the artist and the girl at that moment as they looked at each other, the artist calling her forth, the girl cautiously questioning. A deep meeting was most certainly taking place between them, because as time went on, the girl became less afraid and more trusting. But yet, she did not speak, nor did she smile. Her countenance and manner remained grave and questioning.

The lump of clay, however, had become a bond between them, and now the artist was helping her to work it into more complex forms. She seemed to be trying to shape something that would not come. She became increasingly tense and irritable. Finally, she threw the clay down on the table where they were working and hit it angrily with her clenched fist, then looked at him anxiously. He smiled at her and put his hand over her clenched and angry one. Wonderingly she looked down at his hand on hers as both rested on the shapeless clay; gradually a faint smile softened the anxious hopelessness that had shown on her face for so many months. Reassured, they returned to their work and the artist said, "You see, Jane, I like you and believe in you, so you don't need to worry when things don't go right."

It was then that she spoke for the first time in months. Searching his face, she said wonderingly, "You like me!"

From this time on, her progress was rapid. Before long, Jane was able to talk to her doctors, and little by little they were able to piece together the story of what led to her breakdown. And as we listen to that story, we discover that the difference between Jane and the rest of us is one of degree only.

Her parents, Dick and Julie, had struggled to achieve the financial and social position that was theirs. And they had had great hopes and plans for their older daughter. They loved her, but their anxiety for her to excel in popularity and accomplishment had made her feel that she would be loved only so long as she continued to meet their expectations. Love was not free, she felt. She had to buy it with good behavior and with achievement in those areas that were important to the people from whom she looked for love. When she approached marriage, she brought with her this same concept of love. But so emotionally exhausted was she from her effort to meet the demands of love as she understood them, that she could not face the demands of the marriage love-relationship that lay ahead of her. Quite appropriately, then, on the eve of her marriage, she fled from life and love, and found refuge in illness.

The first lesson of this story is that the personal has power to awaken life, to destroy it, but also to reawaken it. The more we understand Jane's story, the more we understand that the source of our creativeness *is* in love's power to heal and renew. We must make clear immediately, however, what we mean by love. Jane's parents loved her the best they knew how, but their love was possessive in that they expected her to do what they needed her to do. It awakened in her a fear of "love," and she became afraid to face the normal responsibilities and risks of a new love. True love, however, is not self-centered demand; it does not count the cost. True love gives—gives itself. The gift of love is a personal gift and is not made in order to hold or use the loved one. Of course, there is risk in such giving: the risk of little or no return of love; the risk even of rejection; the risk that having loved, the loved one will not love us as we should like, nor be the kind of person who does the kind of things that we like. Jane's parents could not face this risk. They could not give, then trust Jane's response. They tried to make sure that she would respond to their love by meeting their expectations as to the kind of person they wanted her to be and the kind of life they wanted her to live. Their anxiety in giving created in Jane an anxiety in responding. Their anxiety about her became her anxiety about herself.

ii

These risks of self-giving that we have been talking about are really the risks of finding new forms of life, new ways of living—the risk of creativity. New life always seeks new forms. Truth newly perceived, love newly born, beauty newly seen—these always seek new expression. All human achievement is born of this drive of new life to find new form equal to its vitality. And Jane was new life, seeking her way and her forms for living. She was born to be, and she was waiting for the love that would release her power of being. The first cry of Jane, the infant, was the first cry of Jane, the woman, who was already coming into being. What kind of woman would she be? There was within her a drive, an urge, that sent her forth into life to find herself. It was seen in her striving to speak, to form out of the babbling of infancy the words of mature communication. It was seen in her playing with dolls and in her working out with them the pattern of joy and sorrow, of frustration and fulfillment between people. It was seen in her use of blocks and pencils, of scissors and paints, as an attempt to express her creative spirit.

It was seen also in her efforts to respond to, and influence, life. All her living was a response to the summons of her world, a world made up mostly of those who took care of her and loved her. They "educated" her and drew out and released her powers. They encouraged and criticized her and helped her to choose that which was good for her and for all men. She needed her parents and teachers to guide her with as little interference as possible in order that out of rebellion, she not reject them as her helpers and, thus, be led to reject others. Instead, she needed to be called into relation, into communion.

And so do we all. We cannot grow and become persons unless we are willing and able to invest ourselves in living with others. Because there are risks in this, there is also always the question: Are we willing to take these risks? are we willing to abandon the old forms and satisfactions and securities of life for the sake of the new life and relationships that might follow? Of course, the danger is that in that process we may lose the old and not gain the new. Jane failed this test. She dared not invest herself in the relationship of marriage. But the test was failed in the first instance by her parents. They dared not trust their love and Jane's response to it. They tried to guarantee their investment of themselves as parents, and lost. We must not blame them. They, like us, were human. It is human to be creative, and it is also very human to be afraid of the risks of creativity.

When Jane was born, her parents knew, in themselves, the love that she needed in order to become Jane. Their love was meant to be the creative source of their relationship as a family. But when they tried to express their love, they began to have the difficulties that all of us have when we seek to give form to the creative impulse and content within us. There is always the tragic discrepancy between the love we feel and the love we can express, between the dream and its realization, between the brilliance of a thought as conceived and its articulation. There is always the cooling down of the original flame. The results of our efforts to express ourselves are so disappointing as compared with the glory and promise of our visions that we begin sometimes to doubt the vision also. When this happens, we begin to water down hopes and settle for smaller goals.

This is precisely what happened in the case of Dick and Julie. Their personal insecurities and anxieties—which in themselves were not unusual—kept them from being able to express their love in ways that might help their daughter grow and become herself. Instead, they made her a prisoner of their expectations. They could not restrain themselves from building up in their own minds an image of what she should be like, an image corresponding probably to what they wanted to be, but were not. Their image of her demanded that she conform to the patterns set by that image. Because they could not accept her for what she was, they were unable to help her actualize her potentiality as a person. The illness in which she became inaccessible as a person made her the prisoner of that denied self. Her potential self was locked up behind her fears of what people expected of her.

Jane needed genuine help in order to complete the transition from adolescence to maturity, from the filial to the parental roles. But she had not received this and was not able, therefore, to complete the work of growth. The prospect of marriage threatened her, and the love of her prospective husband was experienced by her, as we have seen, as a demand rather than as a gift. The old forms of life as an adolescent were not equal to the vitality of the new relationship, and she did not have the courage to trust the new relationship to help her find new forms for her life. Thus, the only alternative open to her was to retreat back to that point where she would be safe from the demand of life and love. And when she did that, she died as a person and with her perished her creativity.

We must not think that Jane's case is unusual. It is un-

usual in degree only. Many of us experience a similar death
of self and creativity, only to a lesser degree. Our disillusion-
ments and frustrations destroy our hope and confidence.
Even love is not as trustworthy as we had hoped, because
love, contrary to our expectations, seems to promise more
than it can produce. At this point we find it easier to exploit
the personal rather than enter into mutual relations with
persons. And one of the surest signs of our condition is our
relative inaccessibility to one another, a symptom that we
share with Jane. Having failed to actualize ourselves—our
visions, hopes, insights, loves, and plans—we tend to withdraw from each other. We decide to play it safe. Like Jane,
we decide to take what is left and bury it where it will be
safe. Indeed, as was true of Jane and her parents, our
difficulty in expressing the creative love and purpose that
is within us causes us to lose faith in what we are trying
to express so that we lose the creative fire that is necessary
to meaningful living. We have an illustration of part of this
truth in the Parable of the Talents (*Matthew* 25:14-30):
When we become afraid and seek to save our creative
heritage by burying it, we lose it.

Though Jane had fled life, she was brought back; though
she had died as a person, she was made to live again. Can
we understand what happened in such a way that it will
help us to help one another?

Thus far, our consideration of this story has centered
mostly on Jane and her parents. The account of what her
parents did has helped us to realize with what difficulty we
express our love for our own and other children. Like Dick
and Julie, we, too, are sometimes able to see in our own case
how we use our love to seize and control our "loved ones"
and thus stifle their creativity. Like Jane, we sense our
potentialities that have never been actualized, our fear of
the demands of love, and our fear of the risks of loving

another. We, too, have our withdrawals, and there are times with us also, when we cannot hear and respond to the help that might be offered. Likewise, we are able to identify with the frustration of the physicians and chaplain, because we understand how the role of helper is far from being an easy one. Actually, one of the most common experiences in trying to help others is a feeling of helplessness in doing so. We sense that really to help others, we must maintain a patience and persistence that is most difficult to muster and sustain. Then, too, there is the fear that we will fail and that our efforts will be wasted. We also fear that the problems of the one to be helped will involve us more than we are willing to permit. Again there is the fear that the pain of the one needing help will become our pain. In all these respects we find our own place alongside of these very human people, and as we do so, we learn something more about ourselves, our needs, and our hopes.

Now let us look at the artist's role and learn from him, for he, as a person, made his creativity available to Jane— even as we can make ours available to others.

iii
The turning point in Jane's life was the moment when she and the artist met. He found her where she was living in her loneliness and despair, and he led her back to life and love. To find her and bring her back, though, was not easy. She was lost and alone; to reach her, he had to participate in her lostness and deadness, accept her suspicion of him, endure the long weeks of unresponsiveness, and offer love through the unpromising form of a lump of clay. Yet he reached her because of what was in him and what he believed was in her.

He was creative not by reason of his technique as a painter and sculptor, or of his skill in the use of them;

rather because of his belief in, and feeling for, the potentiality of man and nature. He was open to their presence and meaning. He was alert and responsive to life. Within the inertness of clay he could see the possible forms of beauty, and within the deadness of Jane he could see the person she was meant to be. By the power of his creative person he could bring both these together so that the promise of each was released. His technical skills were disciplines by which he expressed his creative relation to life, but they were not the source of that relation. Many people go about the recovery of creativity the wrong way. They think that if they learn the necessary techniques of expression—as, for example, drawing—they will become new persons. The process, however, must be the other way around. Just as the blind cannot transfer to canvas what they see, neither can those whose spirits are unseeing and unresponding communicate anything, regardless of the technical skills they master. The rebirth of persons and their creativity must come from personal, rather than from technical, influences. Technique must always be the servant of the personal. Without the personal, techniques become simply dead form.

The techniques of religion and psychiatry may stand helpless before human sin and sickness when the priest and doctor fail, as a part of their ministration, to give themselves. Therapists at the hospital said that they could not help Jane because she could not hear them. This is the point! When we cannot hear, techniques cannot help us. When we cannot hear, the reason is that it is too painful for us to hear. More than techniques, we need the person himself to break through to us with unmistakable gifts of love and reassurance. Knowledge and skill may be resources in helping the break-through, but of themselves they cannot heal. When religion, for instance, becomes verbal and formal, it loses its power to heal and to reconcile person to person and life to life. Christ makes clear that healing and redemption take place only where there is a personal action. The saving person must participate in a relationship with the person being helped.

The artist did not talk; he acted. He did not use the language of words at first. He went to Jane and dwelled with her, taking upon himself her uncreativity and using his vitality to bear the burden of her deadness. This was the language of that healing relationship. I can hear some of my readers say: "Your imagination and your theology are running away with you. You are making the artist of your story sound as if he were the Saviour. Men do not have this kind of power to heal and to restore."

My answer to this objection is that men do not have to be the Saviour to do saving and healing work. Our Saviour promised that we may do His work and expect to do great things—among them to heal the sick and raise the dead. We do not know the source of the artist's creative power of the personal, but we know that he led Jane back through the dark caverns of her anxiety until she appeared once again responsive to life and love, with her heritage as a person restored to her. We do not know whether the artist was a member of the Church or whether it was as a Christian he helped Jane. But we do know that he was to her what our Lord wants us all to be to one another. The Spirit releases the power of the creative in us in order that by His power we may release the creative powers of others.

In the artist's relation to Jane, then, we see the power of the personal revealed in its re-creating work. He lived a parable of redemption. We see how necessary it is for the saving person, acting out of power of *the* Saving Person, to take upon himself something of the hopelessness and deadness of the one who is being helped. To do this, George

Duncan had to be self-effacing so far as his own needs were concerned. In this he stood in sharp contrast to Jane's parents and the others who had tried to help her because their needs always stood in the way of their doing so. Her parents needed her to be popular and a success. Perhaps the physicians and clergy needed to be successful in their care of her. The artist, on the other hand, was interested only in what she would and could do, and not in his own need to be creative. He was willing to trust her. It was this trust which she sensed and which awakened in her a new trust of the world as a place into which she might make another timid venture. Jane, we note, responded to being esteemed as a person—a response that becomes possible only when one person relates *freely* to another.

In the case of George Duncan, it happened that the artist and the creative person were one. It is not necessary, however, to be an artist in order to be a creative person. George Duncan was primarily a man and, secondly, an artist. As a person, he embodied in himself those qualities and activities needed by Jane.

We saw another instance of this creativity (in Chapter 2) in the case of Joe and his teacher. To help him, Joe's teacher had to have the courage to face him, to be aware of how he was feeling, and to sense what his situation was. She was so really present to him in her direct awareness of his need that she lost completely her timidity. In that moment she was no longer afraid of her responsibility as a teacher or of losing her job. It was only to this kind of courage and awareness that the boy could respond; it alone could summon him from destructiveness to creativeness.

George Duncan was a creative person, however, in a twofold sense. As an artist he had to open himself to his impressions, to allow his vision to mold *him* before he could put it on canvas. As a person, he yielded himself to a similar pattern. In his personal relations he was not seeking to dominate, to find selfish enjoyment, or to exploit. Although his life was torn by the usual human tensions, he was single-hearted in his devotion to life and beauty, and to his discovery and portrayal of them. Some people have this capacity of single-heartedness to a high degree, and they are able to convey it to others by both word and action. They seem to be more completely present to, and aware of, others. Their kindness is clearly recognized as kindness and seems startlingly free of ulterior motives. Their compassion unconfusedly embraces those in need. One responds to them with a renewed sense of life and of its possibilities. Children's fear of the unknown is caught up in their trust of one who meets them with such understanding. The despair of adults over the limiting effect of the past upon their shrinking present is dissolved in the presence of such single-hearted companions. To be touched by this spirit is not only to have one's creativity restored, but also to be able to restore it in others.

Duncan was a person touched by this very spirit. He had not always been such; there was a time when he could not have helped Jane. Truth to tell, during his earlier years, he put on canvas after canvas the grim pictures of his bitterness and distrust. One day he visted a small museum where an older painter belonging to another school was holding an exhibit. During the afternoon he found himself standing before a painting of this artist which was filled with a luminous light that emerged from a small single figure in the foreground. The composition gave the impression that the light was overcoming the darkness, forcing it to recede toward the edge of the picture, and yet, here and there it lurked, held back by the light and yet ever ready to come forward again. Never had George Duncan seen light as a living force so vividly portrayed. He was strangely moved, for he seemed to be witnessing his own rebirth. The figure in the picture *was* the source of the light that drove away the darkness. And yet it came not so much *from* him as *through* him, since he received the light from the radiance around him. Nonetheless, it concentrated in him and, in a very real sense, radiated from him.

For weeks the memory of that painting worked on George Duncan's spirit. Finally, its meaning became clear. The world was full of light, of beauty, of love—of life that could be his if he would but receive it. It would focus in him if he would consent to become its instrument and thus radiate it through his living and painting. This insight of a moment effected in him a marked change. He began to cultivate single-heartedness both as a man and as an artist. As a man, he looked for the locked up creativity in others in order somehow to help release it. This is always the first work of a creative person, whether artist or not. As artist, on the other hand, he began to portray in his pictures the creativity his single-heartedness released. His work became noted for the sense of liberation it revealed. Thus it was that when he met Jane, he was able to see and call forth her lost creativity.

Finally, we see how the creative person is creatively able to use unpromising material to awaken life. Words had not been able to stir Jane. But a lump of clay in the hands of a loving person called her back into being.

Had a lump of clay been sitting beside Jane on the floor, we would never have guessed that it could play an effective role in restoring her to life. And yet, in love's creative hands, it becomes the outward sign of a saving relationship—an instrument of healing. This is what happens when the power of the personal is released to do its reuniting work. It draws men together and catches up the impersonal and material world into the fellowship of persons. Our Lord did this when

He took bread and wine and made it the symbol and instrument of His saving love. The recovery of our creativity
includes the recovery of our relationship with the world of
nature so that our attitude toward, and use of, natural
resources and material things become an outward sign, and
an effective instrument, of our restored relationship.

The artist's recalling of Jane to life by the power of his
acceptance through his use of clay is a kind of sacrament.
It certainly illustrates the sacramental principle of life.
Things may be used as instruments of life—or death—for
the sacramental is a form of communication. In an earlier
work, *Man's Need and God's Action,* I tried to show how
the language of relationships and the language of words
depend upon each other. Now I wish to add to that the
concept of the role of things as instruments of communication. The artist could not reach Jane by words, since she
had been so hurt by people that she had shut herself away
from relationships. So the artist used clay, the person used
a thing. Because it was non-personal, the clay did not
alarm Jane, and it gave the artist creative access to a frightened and hidden girl. Sometimes meaning can be conveyed
by words, sometimes by the lived relationship; but sometimes communication requires more subtle means—a sacramental instrument. Indeed, through the centuries, the
world of things has always been an instrument of the
personal for creative and re-creative activity in persons and
between persons.

iv

Some people, having heard the story
of the artist and Jane, have commented that it is a beautiful story, but not one that helps them with their own loss
of creativity. It is too special, they say. It is about a psy-
chotic girl, and they are not that sick; and about an artist,

and they are not that talented. True enough perhaps, but the point of the story has relevance for all of us: *That the relationship of love is the source of creativity.* This is a tremendous theme in which we all need to believe and participate. The story of Sleeping Beauty, whose life had come to a standstill because of a witch's curse and who was awakened from her long sleep by a Prince's kiss, speaks to us all. We do not reject it because we are neither a princess who has been sleeping for a hundred years, nor the prince come to the rescue. Why then should we not hear, understand, and be helped by the story of Jane and the artist?

We are all concerned about being really alive. More than anything, we dread having lived in vain. The difference between what we have achieved and what we feel we ought to achieve gnaws at us constantly. Our anxiety over this discrepancy destroys our creativity in two ways.

We become so troubled that we just give up the struggle and settle for our nightly session before the television set. This is death. Or, we may become so impatient of our failure to close the gap between what we think we are and ought to be that we sap our creativity by restless, anxious straining against our real limitations as men. This, too, is the way of death. And our illustration-proof of this is the case of Jane who broke under the same pressure: the wife she wanted to become was too much for the girl she was.

Dick Foster, on the other hand, illustrates the struggle that we must put up if we would overcome the obstacles and win some measure of creativeness. *True creativity comes not from the removal of tension but from the acceptance of it.* Dick must be himself and not just a part. To be an adjunct of something, a part of an organization that makes itself the goal of life, such as his business organization or his church, would make him a thing. He is resisting every effort on the part of these to capture him and take away his freedom to be himself. On the other hand, he needs to be a member of a body in as many ways as possible. And as a member, he needs the help of the organism and its members. He needs their belief in him, their encouragement, and their love—even as they need his. He becomes himself as he is helped to accept his limitations and use his powers to relate to others, to act responsibly and decisively. If we take his marriage by way of illustration, we can say that Dick will become himself as he continues to love Julie, act responsibly in relation to her, and make the best decisions he can for their mutual welfare. Faithfulness in this kind of living will be a continuing source of creativity for him and for her, but not without struggle and pain.

Finally, there is the artist, George Duncan, who has made his peace with his limitations as a human being. He has learned to accept and use his resources as a person in the context of his dependence upon others and, likewise, to accept his responsibilities for them. He sees the physical world as an instrument of Spirit. All these have become challenges to his creativity, the means by which he calls forth the creativity of others.

Thus, both Dick Foster *and* George Duncan are examples for us. One is struggling for creativity, the other has found a large measure of it. Both refuse to die as persons, by giving way to the enemies of creativity; and both are seeking to avoid trying to be more than men, sensing that if they try to be like God, they will be destroyed. Both need to love in order to be creative.

This is our clue. The means of creativity is within the reach of each of us. We shall find it, however, only in the way we live our daily relations and assume our present responsibilities. In the next chapter, "What Love Can Do," we shall begin to explore the meaning of this.

4

What Love Can Do

"First stop already. Guess I must have been dozing. There goes the tired businessman. What kind of a wife has he—and kids? There they are—nice-looking family. Kids seem glad to see him and he certainly is crazy about them. Look at the hug he gives the little boy. Wife seems to take it in her stride—all he gets from her is a peck on the cheek. She's got it, too! Isn't any wife glad to see her husband? Yes, this one climbing out of the stationwagon—look at that! Acts as if she hadn't seen him since Christmas, instead of at the 8:17 this morning. Looks about my age, too—what've they got that we haven't? They're important to each other. Love's a funny thing—so easy to turn it into hate or indifference. Is that what Julie and I are looking for—an importance that won't let love turn sour?"

—Dick Foster

4 Something happened to Dick and Julie Foster's love for each other. Dick's thoughts revealed his sense of separation and longing for reunion with her. And Julie, too, suffered from the same sense of separation and longed for reunion with him. She, also, wondered how it happened that they had become such strangers. How impossible, it seemed, that she should feel so cut off from the one to whom she had been so close. Both were suffering because they were lonely, and they were lonely because they could not love. It was love that had first brought them together, and now it was only love that could reunite them. Love, therefore, has real work to do: to call us back into relation with one another.

i

Some of us may be surprised to learn that love is work and has tremendous tasks to perform. We are more likely to think of love as always wearing party clothes and playing glamorously in perpetual sunsets and moonlight. What a surprise to discover that love does some of its most serious work in stained and torn bluejeans in the heat of the day.

We know from Dick's thoughts how anxious he was about their situation. But we do not know as much about Julie's, and it is time we did. When he swept Julie off her feet, Dick had been a gay and earnest young man who seemed to possess a good deal of self assurance, friendliness, and ability. Not long after their marriage, however, Julie began to discover that beneath the surface Dick was really an uneasy person, and lacked confidence in himself and in the impression he made upon others. He seemed to demand a good deal of reassurance from her. He expected many demonstrations of affection and love from Julie, but his expressions of understanding support and affection were restrained and faltering. She then discovered—what so many others have also discovered to their dismay—that the more she gave, the more insatiable Dick became, because he could not really believe that she loved him. Since he could not benefit from her love, he could not love her. And yet all the while, he was expecting their relationship to prosper and was upset when misunderstandings, quarrels, and uncommunicative silences increased.

Julie tried to talk to Dick about these matters, but the effect of her attempts was so painful that she finally abandoned her efforts altogether. Instead, she began to withdraw and become more and more weary and discouraged.

It was about this time that Dick and Julie attended at their church a lecture on marriage sponsored by the Men's Club. Something the lecturer said gave Dick and Julie courage to make an appointment with him to discuss their situation. Dick began by admitting that he had trouble getting along with people. "It's not that I don't like people," he said, "because I really do. But I seem to hurt or offend them in some way. I don't know why—I want to like them, and I want them to like me. For some reason I don't seem to make the grade with people."

When the lecturer asked him what kind of relationship he would like to have, Dick thought a moment and said, "I'd like to feel easy with people and have them feel easy with me. Instead, I feel they are expecting something of me, and that somehow I should do something for them. The closest I ever came to being really comfortable with anyone was with Julie. For the first time I knew what it was not to be lonely. Falling in love and getting married was for me like coming out of solitary confinement after twenty-three years. But the sense of closeness did not last very long. . . .

Judging by your lecture the other night, I counted on my life with her too much. . . . I guess I wanted her to make up for everything I'd never had. If what you said is right, I got married for the wrong reason. You said that marriage can only succeed when the partners enter it with the purpose to give rather than to receive. And it occurred to me that I had really gone into marriage looking for something. No wonder Julie has been so disappointed. She got a raw deal. I expected her to give, but what did I give, in return, to her?"

"That's not the real trouble," interrupted Julie. "The real trouble has been that you would never really let me love you. I think the Doctor here hit the nail on the head when he said that we had to accept love as well as give it. I had already begun to understand, Dick, that you wanted love but couldn't accept it. You always acted uncomfortable whenever I tried to give you anything or do anything for you. . . . I often thought you acted kind of guilty."

"I never thought of it that way."

"Well, I have," continued Julie. "It's been discouraging to want to love you, to see your need of my love, to have you resent it, and be unable to accept my love. The other thing that discouraged me was that you seemed to expect our marriage to come ready-made for us without any effort on our part."

The rest of the conversation between Dick and Julie was important to them, but it is not necessary to record it here. Julie was right. It is hard to love people who cannot accept love. Like Dick, many people are made uncomfortable by having to be dependent upon others for love or anything else. Their resentment of being cared for, in spite of their desire for it, keeps them from benefiting from having been loved. This means, of course, that they, like Dick, are unable to love because the capacity to love depends upon having been loved. Dick apparently felt that it was unmanly to admit to his need of being loved so that he could accept Julie's love. He did not understand that giving and receiving love should work together. When we are born, we need love and care in order to live. When we are loved, we feel good and we respond and, little by little, learn to love. As we grow older, we acquire a new need—the need to love wife, children, and others. But our need to be loved remains with us. Although, in an adult, it should not interfere with the freedom to love.

Thus Julie wants Dick to need her because she needs to love him; and when Dick accepts her love, he becomes better able to love her. The remedy for our problems of love is often already within us: in our being true to our need of love and to our need *to love*. This is the work of love by which we are united and reunited with one another.

Dick and Julie, like many of us, were misled by a superficial conception of love. They naïvely assumed that because they were "in love," the future of their relationship was assured. Because of their strong feelings for each other, they assumed that they were a perfect match. They were unprepared for the eventual discovery that many of their tastes and needs were different and clashed. And each approached the other more with the expectation of being loved than with that of loving the other. Thus, the concept of love with which they began their marriage was not equal to the tasks of their relationship. They had become bewildered by the breakdown of their marriage and did not understand how they had lost each other.

Our first deep need, like Dick and Julie's, is *to be loved*. When Dick and Julie met and "fell in love," their love had to overcome their natural separation of person from person. Each person, endowed with his own particular individuality and, therefore, a separate person, is lonely. His loneliness can be either destructive or helpful. It is destructive when it causes him to sell his individuality short for the sake of a "mess" of companionship. It is helpful when it moves him to respond to it by plumbing more courageously the possibilities of human relationships. Communication is the attempt on the part of two selves to find and to call each other out of the loneliness of independent selfhood into a relationship of mutual interest and purpose. The communication of love alone has the power to reunite the separated.

The establishment of a relationship is not easy. Two individuals are like two impregnable fortresses. They cannot be taken by assault. The center of any individual cannot be wholly entered by any other individual. Even when two people are in love and are open to the possibility of relationship, there is still the difficulty of achieving the union.

The only way in which two people can be really brought together is by the power of love. Only love makes possible a union in which the two persons are each preserved and strengthened. So, when Dick and Julie, as distinct individuals, fell in love, they began to become one. But the question was: Will their individuality help or hinder their union? We need to remember that these two persons have within themselves not only the love that draws them together, but also those things which will separate them.

ii

As we live together, we bring to each other everything that we have and are. Because our experiences in relationship are various, however, we bring not only trust, but also mistrust, of other people. We bring not only our desire for love but our fear of love because some of our experiences with family and friends have hurt us. We bring the resentments toward people that we have accumulated as a result of what we believe to be their injustices to us. We bring our defensive ways of living that help us to keep demanding, hurtful people at a safe distance. We bring our images of ourselves and others, and, using them like puppets, vainly try to act out our concerns. We are afraid to let people see us, and we are afraid to see others really. We put on masks to protect ourselves from being *found out*, although these masks, in reality, keep us from being *found*.

Since we bring these attitudes and ways of response with us to love and marriage, there follows a kind of contest between our love for another and our need to protect our own shaky selves. We put a price on the "love" we would give. It is almost as if we were to say, "I'll love you if you will do what I want." Such bargaining can only separate us from those we love: in the first place, it awakens resentment, not love; and, second, it causes us to hurt our loved ones. Thus we begin to experience another kind of separation—that which arises from our acts of alienation. Now we suffer from double separation: the natural one of two independent selves, and the alienated one of two people who have hurt each other. And love, which is the power of reunion, now has a double task.

There is really nothing unusual in Dick and Julie's experience and condition. Most of us who are in our middle years suffer to some degree the same disillusionment and sense of separation and loneliness. We, too, have abandoned many of our expectations, have settled for a second best, and defend our lovelessness by saying that love is only for the young. We have slowed down physically and mentally beyond the rate that should be expected of us, and we reluctantly admit that we are on the downhill side to the grave. We once believed in love and assumed that because we loved each other, we would have power to overcome our difficulties and would also be equal to our tasks. But, our romantic view of love was broken on the rocks of our needs, our fears, and our guilts.

Is there no place for romance in love? Indeed, there is. Love is infinite in its variations and wears many guises, including those of romantic feelings and sentiments. They do and should play a part in our love life, not only in the beginning but through the years. But it is tragic when the romantic ideal is mistaken for the whole of love because such feelings are not equal to the demands of a life lived together. Dick and Julie's feelings for each other made them happy for a while, but the stresses and strains of their life cast clouds over their happiness and drove away their feelings of closeness.

Each experience of love is always tested. Many people complain because after the achievement of closest union, they experience the real test of their relationship. This was true of Dick and Julie. Each time they knew the joy of fulfillment in their love and their separation was overcome, the new test of love would appear. They, like the rest of us, interpreted these conflicts as the signs of the failure of love and allowed themselves to become discouraged. They did not know that what they had experienced was only the beginning of the full work of love. A love relationship is never static, but changing and growing. We can never say that it has been achieved.

The life of love can be a life of increasing, rather than diminishing, meaning. And it is that for many people. The time came, as we have seen, when Julie was able to speak of the moment in her life when she began to realize that the relationship between Dick and herself did not come to them ready-made because they loved each other. In that moment, she began to see that because they loved each other, they had a relationship in which they might grow together. When we are able to accept our relationships as people who have learned this lesson, we find that the experiences together are both strenuous and strengthening, demanding and rewarding, complicated and simple, frightening and reassuring, stormy and serene, passionate and gentle, ecstatic and plodding, but through it all, triumphant!

In other words, growth in love does not occur automatically. It calls for commitment and effort on our part. Circumstances often require us to make decisions for the real work of love and its strange peace, the peace that passes all understanding; or, for a false kind of love and for its peace-at-any-price. If we choose true love, we will experience pain and suffering, but we will also have the more memorable experience of having loved and lived victoriously.

If we had this concept of the full nature of the experience of love, we would not have had such illusory expectations. We would be more accepting of ourselves and of our experience in love so that when we come to what are supposed to be our creative years, we would not be so tired and discouraged. We might still be living with hope because of our growing faith in love.

iii

But, how can we have faith in love when it seems so ambiguous? We can trust love because "God is love, and he who abides in love, abides in God, and God abides in him." (I *John* 4:16). This is our faith. God and love are one. "God's being is the being of love and God's infinite power of being is the infinite power of love." [1] There is nothing ambiguous about His love. It is constant and enduring even unto the end. The revelation of it in Christ reveals the full nature of the work of love. In His life there

[1]Tillich, Paul, *The New Being*.

is revealed the companionship of His love; in His death, the sacrifice of love; and in His resurrection, the triumph of His love. These three *revelations* belong to each other, and they tell us that if we would love, we must expect these three kinds of experiences. We will have times of warm companionship, times of testing and of separation when we will be tempted to think that love has failed, and times of triumph, of renewal, of reunion.

There is still something else revealed of God's love in Christ. God's love is always love in action. It is action in relation to our pretensions, fears, sins, and needs. And our love in all its expressions is His will. If this is true, we can believe then that the power of God's love is in our ambiguous love. All we need to do is to have faith in His power of love and to surrender ours to Him. If we live in this faith, then we can believe that in every moment of genuine love, we are dwelling in love and God in us, and that the work of love will be accomplished. And, the work that love seeks to accomplish is our union and reunion with one another.

When we view love in this light, it begins to be clear that no one is ever too old for love, for no one ever outgrows the need for union, reconciliation, and reunion. Indeed, love is more necessary for us in our creative years than many of us have allowed ourselves to think, because it is during those years that we are meeting overwhelming demands and having our strength tested by tremendous tasks. We need more than the idea of such a love. We need this love incarnated in our human relationships, expressed in acts of devotion and heroism, in the words of our lips, and in the action of our bodies when appropriately indicated. There is strength and reassurance to be had in every form of love, and it should be available to all men and women at all times.

It is unquestionably true that our deepest need is to be loved; but to give love is our greatest work. Since our need of love and our need to love are so unmistakable, why don't we turn toward each other again with the gift of ourselves and let love work between us once more. But the question is raised, "How can we begin to love again?" "How should we start?" "What shall we do?"

If we would love, we must listen to one another. This is the first work of love. In listening we give ourselves to others, we give them our attention, we commit ourselves to them. Unless two people listen to each other, a relationship cannot grow between them. Each will be a stranger to the other. And, certainly no intimate relationship is possible because intimacy is a relationship at a profound level. At this level, listening must be with more than ears. In the act of love, for instance, one listens with every sense of ear, eye, taste, and touch in order to participate in the mystery of the other. Love is the attempt to see what is in the other person, to know him wholly.

This listening is not a one-sided activity. The other person calls to us in all kinds of ways. He wants to be heard because to be heard is to be known. To be known is to live. Many wives, for instance, are unhappy and complain that their husbands do not love them because their husbands do not listen to them. Inattentiveness has the appearance of disinterest. Of course, wives who chatter aimlessly discourage whatever interest their husbands might have, which brings us to the other side of the responsibility for communication. The husband may want to be attentive, but his wife may so abuse the privilege of speaking that she drives her husband away from her by the abundance and meaninglessness of her words. On the other hand, her excessive talking may be a sign that she is worried because of his preoccupation and "absence," or by her own inability to listen.

Listening as an act of love is a two-sided responsibility, one belonging to the speaker in which she invites listening with worthwhile meaning, and the other responsibility belonging to the listener who seeks to give his whole attention to the person through what is being said. The speaker loves the hearer with the meaning she is trying to convey, and the listener loves the speaker with his single-hearted concentrated attention to her in the moment of communication. When the wife has been heard, and therefore loved (or it may be the husband who has been heard and loved), she may now express her love by listening to her husband, and he by speaking meaningfully to her. He who listens loves, and he who speaks loves. And love gives each the grace to reverse roles by becoming speaker instead of listener, and listener instead of speaker.

Only when a man and woman are really present to each other in this way, is a love relationship possible, and love is the power that enables people to be really present to each other. And certainly marriage without this mutual presentness and versatility is an impossibility.

Dick is going to have to listen to Julie and, in his listening, to try to get behind the image that he has of her and of the image that she has presented of herself. If he succeeds in really hearing her and encouraging her to reveal herself to him, she may acquire the courage to respond once more. And a part of her response will be to begin to try to hear Dick and to be really concerned about what he is trying to reveal to her. In their listening and speaking to one another, they will begin again the work of love, and in beginning it, they will open themselves to each other.

This brings us to the second work of love: *If we would love, we must be responsible for one another.* Sometimes responsibility for others is misunderstood to mean living their lives for them as when a father, out of concern for his son's welfare, makes decisions for him in areas in which his son could and should make them. Not only is the father exercising a mistaken kind of responsibility, but he is also failing to express his love. Responsibility as an act of love means living our own lives in ways that will help others to live theirs. According to this principle, the father will try to help the boy make his own decision, stand by him as he works it out, give help where needed or asked for, and allow him freedom for making his own mistakes. Likewise, in the marriage relationship, each partner expresses love by trying to live so that the other is helped to live his life.

The mature person loves because he has been loved and because his love of others has been accepted by them. Gradually it has become his nature to love so that at times it can be said he loves not because he has been loved or hopes for return of love but because his love is needed. He accepts and exercises his responsibility to love others, even when he has no feelings for them. He employs the power to love to increase love especially where and when it is needed most. Dick and Julie now have a chance to employ whatever power of love they have to meet one another's need of love. This is their responsibility. For instance, Julie undoubtedly would like him to be responsive to her, but she must awaken his responsiveness by living her love for him. Many of us are tempted to rebel against this concept of love because we are used to thinking of love as something we receive rather than give. If Dick and Julie should continue to think of love the way they did, there would be no hope for them. They could only become more estranged and lonely. But if either of them could give love for the sake of the other, the love response of the other would be awakened, and the vicious circle of demand and resentment that now separates them broken.

Love as responsibility must be shown for our beloved's interests and needs. And those who love us will exercise, in turn, responsibility for ours. A responsible husband, for instance, is alert to his wife's need. To the extent that he cares for her, she is relieved of the necessity of looking after herself. Indeed, he can do a better job of it than she can. When she calls attention to her needs, he may experience her need as a demand. She may be so concerned about herself that she becomes inattentive to him. But to whatever degree he can minister to her, he is more alive and stronger for giving love, and is saved somewhat from experiencing her need as demand. When she becomes alert to his needs, the same becomes true of her experience. Indeed, out of this kind of love, love as mutual responsibility, does love grow.

Another occasion on which love as responsibility may show itself is when a relationship is endangered by the offense of one of its partners. When this happens, one of two responses is possible. Either the other partner may point an accusing finger and thus place the full blame on the "guilty" one. Or, out of love, he may seek to determine what part he may have played in causing the other to offend.

Some years ago when a middle-aged executive invested money that was not his with the hope of a quick return, the bottom fell out of his investment, and he both lost the money he had taken and failed to get the money he needed for his debts. Furthermore, he lost his job, was estranged from his family, and was sent to prison. His wife was violently critical of him even though she made constant references to her great love for him. When she went to her minister for comfort, he was able to help her see that she had been partly responsible for her husband's disgrace because of her extravagant demands, and that if she really loved him, she would accept her part in what he had done.

By the time the husband was paroled, both of them were able to share the responsibility for their trouble and to resume their life again.

Being responsible for one another is our only hope for the renewal of love. Unless each stays with the other regardless of how difficult the situation is, he cannot do anything constructive about it. Don and Phyl, a younger middle-aged couple, came for counseling as a last resort before initiating proceedings for the divorce they felt to be inevitable. After a long, and apparently unsuccessful, discussion of their difficulties, it was suggested to them that, for the sake of the children at least, they return home and try for six months to live together on a different basis. Their new aim was to try to overlook the things in each other that had been irritating them, to strive to see and understand each other as persons, and to be responsible for one another's interests and needs.

This demanded of them considerable maturity, and in the light of their past life, there was little indication that they would be able to supply it. They were able, however, to see at once that one source of their mutual irritation had been the fact that each had formed for himself a picture of what he wanted the other to be. To mention only one example of this mutual irritation, Phyl wanted Don to be more outgoing and scintillating in his social life. His quiet and somewhat shy manner embarrassed her because she needed people to think well of her husband. She would criticise him for being socially lazy and made sly fun of him in public, all of which caused him to be more reserved than ever.

When they made their six-month attempt to live their love on another basis, Don began to look at Phyl's attitude toward his behavior from the point of view of what it meant to her. Then it was that he saw her love for him as well as her dissatisfaction with him. He also saw that she had been trying to make him into the person she needed him to be. He became interested in what her need was and decided that she needed him more than she needed her image of him. As these insights began to be clear to him, he became better able to love her. As he began to love her, his behavior toward her changed accordingly. At the same time, Phyl became aware of Don's growing understanding of her and of his steady, dependable patience not only with herself but with the children and others as well. In time it dawned on her that he was a better man than the one she tried to force him to be. As they began to see each other as they were, love was reawakened in them and reunited them in a relationship that continued to grow. If they had not exercised love as responsibility, however, they would never have known the deeper meaning of love, and the joy and fulfillment that can result from meeting personal trouble with the power of love.

The third work of love is our acceptance of one another. Many people think that when we accept someone, we are called upon to give a blanket approval to everything that he may do. This is not acceptance, but rejection. The delinquent needs to be accepted, but acceptance means dealing with him as a person in ways that might help him to overcome his delinquency. To love another does not mean that one has to like everything about the other. A partner in a relationship may do something unacceptable, and yet, acceptance of him by the other is possible. A husband said of his wife who was an alcoholic, "I hate her alcoholism, but if I am to love her, I must love her as one who for the time being seems to need to be an alcoholic." This is acceptance.

Real acceptance of one person by another is a deep and

difficult event. Unfortunately, many people, because of a superficial understanding of what acceptance is, talk about accepting others as if it were easy. It was not easy for the husband to accept his wife as a woman who was an alcoholic since so much of her behavior while under the influence of alcohol embarrassed and inconvenienced him. Many times he had to make excuses and cover up for her. And even though he knew that she was sick, her inability to meet her responsibility to him and their relationship hurt him. His love for her meant that he would have to accept her for what she was; while at the same time, he tried to help her recover from her illness.

Acceptance must start, of course, from the side of the acceptor; in the case above, the husband. One reason why it is hard to accept others is that there is a primary difficulty of accepting oneself. The husband must accept himself if he is to accept his wife. This means that he must know himself to be fallible and also in need of forgiveness. If he can say, "I have left undone those things which I ought to have done, and I have done those things which I ought not to have done," then he will have the grace and understanding to extend to her real acceptance and forgiveness. The sense of having been forgiven will give him that renewed sense of being loved which becomes, in turn, the source of his power to accept his wife. And his love is one instrument of God's love and acceptance of her.

Thus, love gives this acceptance, even when it has been offended or hurt. The loving one offers the gift of acceptance to the one from whom the offense comes. Through the gift of acceptance, love seeks to mend and renew the broken relationship. And even though it may be broken, the lover keeps it intact within his own heart. He keeps it alive within himself. If Dick Foster, for instance, really wants to do the work of love in relation to Julie, he will have to take the initiative and live their relationship for her until she can. He will have to accept her despair about her marriage and be devoted to her (live with her as though she were devoted) until such time as her devotion is renewed, if ever. In other words, he will have to hold within himself, and for her, the image and the meaning of their marriage. To do this he will have to accept his own lacks and know himself to be forgiven for what he cannot do for her.

This work of love in the form of acceptance is something we are always having to do, and it is not as unusual as it may seem to be at first. At one time or another, a partner has to be strong for the other, but the day comes when, in turn, the second partner has to be strong for the first. Now Dick has to have faith for both of them. Some future day Julie will have to be strong for him.

The prospect of this task of life seems too great for us, and yet none of us has to accomplish love's work alone. If we will let him, the Spirit of Love will dwell in us and give us strength for what we have to do. The perfect love and forgiveness of God seeks to work through our imperfect loves, acceptances, and forgiveness.

iv

Finally, if we would love, we must believe in love, believe in the power of love to reunite people and heal them. Love without great expectation is not love. By its very nature, love has to triumph. Hatred and resentment always fail, but love always prevails.

But many who read these words will protest that love doesn't always succeed. "Look at our lives! Don't they prove that love fails like everything else. The illustration of Dick and Julie Foster is evidence of the failure of love. How can you say that love is victorious?"

We can say that love always wins because of our faith. And

our faith is simple: God, who is Love and whose Spirit works in our lives, seeks to meet our needs to love partly through our love of one another. Thus, we can believe that, though our love is ambiguous, in every moment of genuine love, we are dwelling in God and God in us. Thus, we can believe that love can heal and make alive again. God will use every act of love that is offered Him to heal the lonely and the hurt. To love is to cooperate with God. If we will offer Him each act of love, no matter how imperfect it is, He will use it to accomplish His purpose.

Our disbelief in love is not the result of an experience of love, but of some other kind of experience that pretended to be love. A young woman, who had been married nine years and was determined to leave her husband, said, "I hate love. It has messed up my life. I don't want anything more to do with it." It was not an experience of love that provoked her bitter witness against love. It grew out of a relationship with a husband who said he loved her but who dominated her to the point where her very selfhood was being denied. She was the victim of a domination that had disguised itself as love.

But, someone else speaks up and says, "I have really loved my husband. I've given him myself, my care, and my body unreservedly and gladly, but he cheated on me! How can you say that my love is victorious? Love is a lot of bunk!"

Our response to this protest is, first, that we cannot assume that the expression of her love was as true as she might think. Her love and ours may be sincere and all else that we may say about it, but the expression of it may not be consistent. For instance, are we sure that we have not been beating our partner over the head with the purity of our concept of love, threatening them, indirectly if not directly, should they show any unfaithfulness? It is true that we may drive our partners to violations of the relationship by the way in which we live. Or, we may, by our attitude or action, prevent our partners from straying. One woman whose husband's business involved him in many relations with glamorous women said that she regarded it as her responsibility to help her husband be faithful. If he strayed, it would be as much her fault as his. Her business was, she added, to be the kind of woman that would make it difficult for him to wander. Finally, she said, "We live in a world in which I know that other women will sometimes try to seduce my husband. It is my duty and pleasure to out-seduce them!" Here is love that assumes its responsibility, accepts the nature of man and the immorality of the world, and has faith in the triumphant power of love in all of its expressions. In other words, we must always exercise our love and its expression in such a way and with such intention that we are truly loving and not doing something else under the guise of love.

"But, suppose her husband strayed? Isn't this a sign that love has failed?" you persist in asking. No! One thing true love does not do is to take away the other's freedom. If our relationship has taken away the freedom and independence of our partner, then the relationship is not one of love. And the freedom must include the freedom to stray, to violate the relationship. When this occurs, love has two things to do: First, to continue to love the one who has acted against love, by seeking to destroy the desires and attitudes inimical to it. Second, to awaken in their place attitudes and feelings of love through the forgiveness of all that is against love. This is not easy. In the process, the person who is doing this work of love will suffer and recoil from what seems to be the injustice of his situation. But this is a part of the work of true love. The cross of Christ reveals that love must expect this kind of experience when it accepts its responsibility to heal and reunite person and person.

"Love does not take away another's freedom," we have said. This does not mean that the loved one can do as he pleases. Freedom is not license—license to play fast and loose with love. If we act against love and betray one who loves us, we will suffer estrangement because love has an integrity which it cannot deny. This had happened to Dick and Julie Foster years before when Dick had had an affair with another woman. Julie was outraged and hurt. Her response was to express her love as sorrow, anger, and bitterness. Dick had changed the relationship. Instead of being one between lover and beloved, it had become one between betrayer and betrayed. Both of them suffered because the laws of relationship which lie at the heart of love had been broken. They were estranged. Dick could do no more than say, "I am sorry, forgive me," and try again to live by the rules of love. It is hard to live under the demand of the law of love without the help of love, and Dick felt the burden of it. But this was his *repentance*. It could prepare him for forgiveness but could not effect it. He could not mend the brokenness. Only Julie had the power to mend. She could do so by remembering her own offenses against love, by accepting (which emphatically does not mean approving) Dick's acts against their love and by covering his act with her love. And this was her *forgiveness*.

But their relationship could not be restored to what it was before. In any crisis we want to go back to paradise, back to the relationship as we remember it, forgetting the conditions that originally caused the trouble. In any event, we can never go back; we can only drift or go forward.

Dick and Julie look forward to a new relationship of which the experience of brokenness is a part. But they will have to accept a responsibility for their situation and be willing to bring to it the resources of their faith and love. Love's forgiveness and healing will make their relationship —with all of its brokenness—new and will give it a depth and power it did not have before.

This is what the rest of the Christian story reveals. The love that seemed to go down in defeat triumphed over sin and death in the Resurrection. And so we believe that our love, when we offer it to God, to be the instrument of His love, in spite of every indication to the contrary, will be victorious. Sometimes we will have to accept the possibility that we may not see the evidence of the victory in the lives of those we love or in the desired changes in our relationship, although a part of the work of our love will be to keep us open to the possibilities of change in others. But the victory of love can always be seen in the life of the one who is faithful in the work of love. He may be sad, but he will have the peace that passeth understanding. He will be compassionate and forgiving; he will be open to relationship with God and man. He will be able to rejoice in the sense of self-acceptance that love gives, and out of that self-acceptance gain the courage and poise to face creatively the problems of life even though he may never find any human solution to some of them.

"So faith, hope, love abide, these three; but the greatest of these is love." (*I Corinthians 13:13*)

There is no joy like the joy experienced by two people whose love enables them to face the problems of their life and to emerge on the far side of them with their relationship strengthened and deepened. The great love is not the love that has known no strife, but the love of two people who have come through storms, battered to be sure, but knowing that nothing can separate them from the love of God and therefore from their love of each other. Here is a new and appropriate purpose for the middle years to replace the old purpose of youth, a new excitement of accomplishment, and a new passion for living. We can now expect our love to do a great work, and our expectation should be without fear. Thus, our middle years can become our best years because they are our most creative years.

CHAPTER 5

The Role of Sex in Love

"We rarely make love to each other. When we do try, it doesn't come off very well. . . . It's so damned complicated. Sex used to be a part of our lives. Now it's incomplete and infrequent. It used to bind us together. Now it stands between us . . . divides us . . . makes us enemies. Each of us needs the other, two halves of a whole. Wonder how it happened that we have to justify sex."

—Dick Foster

5 Somehow, through the years, Dick and Julie Foster had lost touch with each other and became, apparently, unable to talk with each other about those things that were important to them. In a sense, they were not living together but rather living parallel lives, side by side, that now and then superficially touched.

When they were married twenty-four years ago, they little dreamed that their life together would end this way. As a matter of fact, they had promised each other never to allow anything to separate them, but separated they became. And as the years passed, the patterns of separation became more rigid and harder to break.

We know that both of them now want to find their way back to each other. Already Dick has some awareness of how his needs have made it harder for Julie. And Julie, on her side, has begun to realize that her turning her back on those needs did not help matters. Each has received some help by talking to a marriage counselor, and both have begun to see that each can help the other more than he does. They have begun to resist the fatalism of some of their friends who are also having marital difficulties and joke about them, half ruefully, half bitterly. These friends assume that nothing can be done about old marriages, that disillusionment and alienation is normal for modern marriage.

This is not a true assumption. But the question does arise: How can we rekindle the flame of an old relationship? In answering this question, we shall consider in this chapter, the role of sex, and in the next chapter, some of the principles of marriage, by applying which we may hope to change the old patterns.

i

Why do we begin our search for the answer with a consideration of the subject of sex? After all, Dick and Julie have been married for twenty-four years, and, as many of their friends would say, they have lived together long enough to have had their "fun." So, why should they be overly concerned that they don't have much sex any more? And, they would ask, why should anyone writing a book about marriage and people in their middle years stress the importance of sex?

The answer is simple and has to do with our natures. Every man and woman is an embodied spirit. For this reason, no real communication can take place between person and person unless the body comes to the aid of the spirit, and the spirit moves the body. The thoughts of another person, which are spiritual in nature, cannot come to me except through the physiological action of his body, focusing in the act of speech. Traveling over air waves, his thoughts are received by my body's delicate mechanisms of hearing, and influence my thought and action.

The fact that we are embodied spirits also underlies the meaning of sex. Love is a thought, a feeling, a sentiment, an aspiration, a determination, that seeks to communicate itself, but, in doing so, is dependent upon the body. Therefore, we have the handclasp of a friend; at the time of feeding and bathing we have communion and communication between mother and child; and we have the kiss of lovers. Ultimately, in the deepest and most complete relationship between man and woman, union is accomplished through the act of sexual intercourse. This is a physical act, to be sure, but it is more than that, and if it isn't more than a physical act, it is not love. One of the best statements on this relationship comes from the former Archbishop William Temple: "Sex belongs to the realm of personal relationships and is the point at which spiritual and physical come into closest interplay."

We can see, therefore, that sex is not only important, but that it is also necessary. Further, it will remain necessary as long as the body is a vehicle for the expression of love. The bodies of both Dick and Julie still need to be the instruments of their love, and their love needs the help of their bodies, even though they have been married for twenty-four years. A human being, for as long as he lives, remains psychosomatic, which is our modern term for body-spirit interdependence. To be sure, the needs, desires, tastes, and energies of people change over the years. But, the changes do not mean that the activities of the body as the instrument of the spirit cease.

Naturally, the interests and activities, spiritual and physical, of a couple in their youth are not the same as those of the same couple in their middle and later years. Both spirit and body change, but, in a love relationship, they change together. Spirit renews and uses the body, and the body, unless incapacitated by disease and accident, remains an able servant of the spirit.

Whatever the age of a couple, the purpose of the relation between the spiritual and physical is that the physical be the outward and visible expression of the inner spirit. Breakdowns in relationship are due more to failures of the spirit than to failures of the body.

As we have seen, only love can reunite the separated. The power of love is the power of life. What, then, is the role of sex in love? Sex and love are commonly associated together. "Making love" is a phrase by which most people refer to the sex act. If sex and love are related and if love has the power to unite individuals and to reunite the separated, then sex has the power to help us break out of our isolation.

Dick's protest against the absence of sex relations with Julie was a part of his anguish over their separation; and her coldness was a symptom of her despair over it. They both want more than the union of their bodies. They want to discover, and rediscover, the union and completion of their respective persons.

Actually, the possibility of intercourse exists as a potential resource for their troubled marriage. In addition to the procreative purpose of sex, there is the re-creative one which has two functions: First, to be the outward, visible sign and expression of any reunion that may be achieved between partners. One experiences this very commonly when, after an experience of oneness in playing, working, or worshiping together, a couple may want to seal this experience of union in an act of physical love. Second, sex may be the physical instrument by which the two partners seek to break through separateness, a purpose for which other means may not seem equally effective. Here the physical unity and intimacy is sought with the frank hope that by it each may find the other as a person. This function of the sexual relationship is legitimate in the context of a marriage where the partners have made a full commitment to each other. These two functions of sex indicate that a marital relationship without the sexual is incomplete and is ignoring a resource for renewal and reunion.

This meaning of sex for the married couple is just as legitimate and important as its procreative meaning. Sex is given to be a means of re-creating the relationship of two people who love each other. It helps them to establish the community upon which society and the children of the union must depend.

Then, there follows the procreative purpose of sex. This comes second because the children of a marriage are dependent upon the quality of relationship into which they are born. Therefore, sex as a means of establishing and adorning the relationship is justified. But the partners of a marriage must also face their procreative responsibilities lest they use sex as a purely selfish means. Thus, the recreative and procreative objectives of sex belong together. The purpose of one is to unify; the purpose of the other, to multiply. The attempt to justify sex relations by referring them to the purpose of reproduction alone is to deny the full God-given purpose of sex, including sex as a means of building a relationship.

ii

Many difficulties complicate these roles of sex. One of the principal difficulties is that we sometimes mistake sexual attraction for personal love. We need to realize, however, that while sex is much more universal and fundamental than marriage, we cannot on that basis equate sexual desire and love; and we need also to realize that both love and sex need the framework of marriage. Before there is marriage, there is sex; and the meaning of marriage depends in part on the meanings that the partners bring out of their sexual development and experience. Here we should make clear that the phrase "sexual experience" does not mean sexual intercourse, and anything said in this chapter may not be interpreted as a justification of premarital sexual intercourse.

We would be blind, however, if we were to conclude, as many do, that a person's sexual experience begins with marriage. We often fail to help children because we tend to think of sex only in relation to marriage. We overlook the fact, and the meaning, of the sex development and experience of children during those years when marriage is only a remote possibility. Even babies have erotic feeling, and children feel sexual attraction and respond variously to their sexual curiosity. Adolescents undergo physiological and anatomical changes that produce sexual feelings and drive them to various kinds of sexual experimentation. All of this is nature's preparation of them for sexual life, for love, and for marriage. The question is: Can we accept this aspect of our own and others' lives? And will we help them with it?

Many of our young people are prevented from achieving a whole and holy sexual relationship because of our inadequate grasp of what is going on in them and because of our refusal to help them to understand the meaning of it. Even when it would be appropriate to deal with sex and marriage together, we often talk about marriage in ways that evade the responsibility of talking intelligently and helpfully about sex. Part of the difficulty is that we are afraid of sex. Yet foolish is the man who does not respect its power for either good or evil, either in marriage or out of it! Too many of us—parents, teachers, and ministers—are afraid to deal with this subject except as we may vaguely refer to it when talking about marriage. Young people and adults, too, need as much as anything a demonstration of an attitude of acceptance of sex as a part of life and of its fundamental purpose and meaning. Along with this there is a need for a group in which people will feel free to ask questions about sex that concern them. There is excellent literature available which may be suggested by ministers, teachers, physicans, and by marriage and mental hygiene clinics, to any individual or group who may wish to study the subject. And most communities have some kind of leadership available for groups or classes that might want to come together to study sex, love, and marriage and to learn how they can help their children and themselves in these areas of life.

Although sex is primary and universal, having meaning in itself apart from marriage, sex expression and life needs marriage to add to its meaning. Sex needs marriage, and marriage needs sex. Sex without marriage has meaning; but its meaning, without the structure and discipline that marriage can provide, is insecure and likely to be transient. This is the point at which many young people need help. They are rightly sure that their relationship calls for sexual expression, but they do not see just as clearly that their sex relationship requires the dependability and continuity of marriage if its meanings are to be preserved and grow.

The power of sex is partly due to the sexual division of creation. The world of sex is a divided world. There is the male who is not complete within himself, and the female who is not complete and sufficient in herself. Male and female were not created to exist separately and in isolation, but created for union and communion. Woman was made to complete man, and man to complete woman, anatomically, biologically, emotionally, mentally, and spiritually. Thus, the power of the sex drive springs from the longing of the incomplete being for completion. The separation is intolerable, and a divided creation groans and suffers, longing for union and fulfillment. The union longed for, however, is more than sexual. It is a longing for a personal union of which the sexual is but a part and not the whole.

The differences between the sexes may be divisive and cause trouble as well as serve to complement and effect completion. Man and woman both have advantages over the other because each possesses that which the other does not have and yet needs. Sometimes we may be tempted to withhold from, or give ourselves for the sake of power over, the other. Or, we may withhold ourselves because of resentment and a desire to punish the other. When we succumb to this temptation, we are participating in a war between the sexes, increasing the enmity between man and woman, and blocking our own relationship. This is what Dick and Julie have been doing, despite the love that originally brought them together.

iii

As we talk together about sex, love, and marriage, it becomes more and more apparent that however unclear some of us might be about the many different purposes that brought us together, back of it all is the deep desire to be united in love and to be healed of whatever brokenness may be ours. This longing of the human soul causes us to put more faith in our love for each other than our capacity for giving and receiving love can later justify. Our need to believe in love sometimes leads us to deify romance. When we base our marriage on this illusion and it fails, our disillusionment is great, and our resulting despair about marriage makes it all the harder to do anything about it. For this reason many people run from one relationship to the next, looking for love. They escape from the failure of one relationship into the deceptive promise of the next. The end is to lose faith in love. It is a natural step from losing faith in man's love to losing faith in God's love. In the beginning, Dick and Julie came together with a faith in love. In so many words and in other ways, they said, "Love can do anything." They had the beginnings of a true faith, but they lost it.

Sexual love, or any form of human love, is not able to meet the whole of human need. When human love seeks to achieve its own fulfillment, there is aspiration, hope, and determination on the part of the lovers. The desire to be at one with each other and to express that oneness in the sex act is the attempt on the part of each to break out of separation and to achieve union. The act to many people seems to re-create them and recall them from loneliness and hostility. Indeed, the experience of sexual intercourse is such that those who participate in it have a partial sense of being "new creation," of "reunion," "purification," and "completion." In a superb paragraph, a poet and theologian describes the significance of the union of man and woman:

"There is here enacted, above all, the ultimate outgoing of man from himself into the waiting depths of being. He descends and plunges into the world 'beneath' and 'above' himself, into the breath of the morning of creation, into the dawn of being. It is the moment, where in awestruck trembling, life transcends its limits. The womb of the world is pierced, and through the narrow crater of a tremendous act, are, as it were, perceived a new 'beneath' and a new 'above,' a 'new earth' and a 'new heaven.' It is the mystery where heaven sheds itself on man, and man yields to heaven; the mystery of the breaking down of all the limits and limitations of human life and isolated human existence, of the petrified and stagnant flesh of man. It is the mystery of a sudden merging and union into a single indivisible being of flesh and spirit, of heaven and earth, of human and divine love. The divine spirit touches human flesh, since it is transparent to Him on its primeval depth, and indeed receives Him in the burning moment of erotic ecstasy. We are witnessing to a true sacrament: the Spirit of God invades the cosmic element, without ceasing to be Spirit, and the flesh widens into the transcendence of the Spirit, without ceasing to be flesh." [1]

The meanings of this insight for attitudes toward sex are clear. In the first place, lust is an offense against the relation-

[1] E. Lampert, *The Divine Realm* (*London:* Faber and Faber, 1944).

ship because it enslaves us and takes away our freedom to love another. Exploitation of the flesh in violation of the spirit does not fulfill the participants but destroys them. It is usually followed by feelings of uncleanness, incompleteness, and guilt. On the other hand, the opposite offense against the relationship is the attitude which seeks to spiritualize the physical out of love, as if love is pure in proportion as it is free of physical expression. A part of the great gift of God to man is that man and woman in married love may come together freely and unashamedly in the communion of the flesh and the spirit in an experience of re-creation.

It might seem from this, and, indeed many people think, that in order to find escape from separation, they need only to love each other and to continue to come together in the sex act. We live in a time when the saving power of love has been rediscovered, and so we assume that in order to be saved we need only to love. The difficulty is that while we have rediscovered the saving power of love, we have not discovered the love that has the power to save. A moment ago we saw that when human love seeks to achieve its own fulfillment, there is aspiration, hope, and determination expressed, but these are sometimes followed by failure, frustration, and despair because, no matter how fulfilling our moments of union and reunion are, there is always the unexperienced and unexpressed love for which our innermost being longs but cannot receive or bestow.

So the truest love story tells of both ecstasy and tragedy, reunion and separation. While we can tolerate tragedy in love stories or in the lives of other people, we find it unacceptable in the love drama of our lives. "Why can't we perfectly love those whom we love?" is a question often heard in one form or another. The reason is that our need of love is greater than our ability to give it. Our need of love and our limited power to love may combine so as to cause frustration and resentment in a marriage. This experience may plunge the couple from the occasional heights of union at one time to the depth of separation and despair another time.

When these times of disillusionment come, a couple may be so disappointed in each other that they tend to reject each other altogether, their assumption being that if they cannot measure up to each other's ideals or expectations perfectly, they do not measure up at all. The "whole loaf or none" attitude is not only unworkable but it is poor theology.

Essential to a happy and growing marriage is a sense of optimism about what one *is* and a sense of need about what one *is not*. Insofar as I am able to love, despite my limitations, I *have* the power of love! Insofar as I am not able to love, I am in need of a power to love that is beyond the power I have. But a limitation in my power to love does not deny the presence of such power to love as I *do have*. Dick and Julie have some power to understand, to forgive, and to help one another. This is the power to love that they do have. But neither of them has the power to love the other perfectly. Hence, each must guard against expecting from the other that which he does not have.

In the marital relationship, therefore, as in every relationship, we live affirmatively in relation to what each is and has for the other, and we avoid demanding of each other that which it is impossible for the other to give. While so doing, however, we need to remember (as if we could ever forget) that that which we cannot give each other, each needs. But the other does not have within himself the wherewithal to meet the demand. Married couples without resources other than those they have in themselves go round and round in an ever deepening circle of frustration and despair. And the sex life of such couples, needless to say, shares in this vicious circle.

Human love, including its sexual expression, needs the enabling power of divine love. Every experience of love, in spite of its incompleteness and sinfulness, points to perfect love. Every reunion accomplished by our love, whatever its expression, crys out for blessing and completion by the eternal love of the Father. It is God's love—*agape*—that the man and woman, out of their individual separateness and brokenness, often unknowingly are seeking. Their love for each other is able to reach toward *agape* but not grasp it. But while men cannot reach God, God can reach man. Divine love, acting through man, is able to give power to human love to accomplish its purpose. This means that the sex act between a husband and wife who love each other becomes an instrument of salvation for them. This is true because they love each other, because God loves those who love one another, and because He works through human love. It is the purpose of God that the relationship of sex which He created should be a means of grace, an instrument for our union and reunion of both body and soul.

As we have seen, Dick Foster's protest against the infrequent and unsatisfying sex relations with Julie was outspoken. Julie's protest was hidden in the twisted corridors of her frustrations. Each of them, in his own way, have raised the question which torments thousands of people in their middle years whose bodies are no longer instruments of love, but ever increasingly the infirm victims of their very resentments. And yet, it may be possible for them to recover for themselves the sacrament of human love so that they may find each other again in the profoundest and most intimate communion given to man and woman.

$\dot{iv}$

How can men and women free themselves from the patterns that separate them? To answer this question, we must turn to the four principles of love with which we ended the last chapter, and apply them to the sex relationship.

The First Principle: *We must listen if we would love.* Much sexual alienation and ineptitude between couples is due to their insensitivity to each other. Sex desire can make us blind and deaf to everything but the satisfactions of our desire, and to every consideration but ourselves. We must resist this danger with every resource we have. And if we have succumbed to this temptation and ruined our sex relationships, we will want to become aware of one another as persons. Love can turn our desire into a passion to give; and, in loving and satisfying the other, be satisfied. One way of doing this is by listening, by being sensitive to the need and possible response of our partner.

The frigid woman, for example, may have been made so by an unobserving, indifferent, insensitive husband. And the woman who seems no longer interested in having sex relations may have retreated in order to protect herself from the sexual indifference or manipulations of her husband. She can be reawakened by an attentive, loving partner. Even though she is older and may have passed through the change of life, still she is capable of being a responsive, capable partner to the husband who really loves her. He will have to pay attention to the rhythms of her physical drives and try to make love to her when she is more inclined to do so. He will try to awaken her by appealing to her mind and emotions as well as her body, and in doing so, listen to whatever indications she makes that might tell him how to reach and awaken her. He must listen with every sense he has for every communication she may give. And she, too, must listen to her husband that she may know how to love him. Many husbands are impotent because the wife did not listen to what her would-be lover tried to tell her over the years. Such a wife may have been uncaring in her response to her husband's physical expression of his love. Instead of meeting him honestly as a woman can and should, she may have hid behind the false idea that she should not show interest and pleasure in intercourse. This is one area in which a wife often does not hear correctly what her husband is trying to tell her through the language of the body, and the area in which husbands really feel misunderstood. Years of this kind of non-communication between two people whose potentiality for communication is so great, produce an emotional turmoil of fear, guilt, and inferiority in which both lose the power to love.

We might think such a couple would have reached the point where they could no longer help themselves. So it would seem, looking at them from the outside. But one must not overlook the power that resides in people in the form of their need for love and their need to love. The fires of human love may be smothered or banked, but they rarely go out. Though they may have smouldered for years, they can burst into flame again when fanned by any evidence of repentance and effort to love. And once love comes alive, it begins to overcome the obstacles to relationship and to reunite even those who seemed unreconcilable. We are not as helpless and lost as some would have us think, even though our situation looks as if we are. When we make a positive effort to love and to forgive, we ally ourselves with the power of God's love which is always at work to unite and reunite us with one another and with Him.

When they turn to each other, therefore, and try, with as little fear and prejudice as possible, to listen to each other's words and actions, they may begin to come together again. They may begin to renew their power to love. Both frigidity and impotence, so prevalent among couples in their middle years, are more often the result of fear and guilt than of any physical condition. Where such conditions exist, the partners are self-conscious and defensive and each thinks more about himself than the other.

Thus, the first step toward changing these conditions is for each to be alert to the other. By our loves listening to the needs of each other, and by rightly hearing the language of the body expressing the message of the person, we may be able to restore to each other the physiological readiness and capability for intercourse.

The Second Principle: *We must accept our human sexual nature and the kind of relationship that nature calls for.*

Sex is a gift of God to both men and women, and just as much a gift to women as it is to men. During these middle years, the sex life of many couples dies because they have reaped the destructive reward of an earlier teaching that sex is for the man and the woman has to make the best of it. The marriage often is also victim of years of ignorance, on the part of both, about the difference between a woman's and a man's response. Some men, for instance, fail to so woo and awaken their wives that they are ready emotionally and physically for intercourse. Treated this way, wives often feel assaulted by the impatience of the man's passion. They may never experience the responding passion and release that come to women who are truly loved and prepared for love. It is no wonder that the sex life of many marriages is either non-existent or troubled and unsatisfying.

But, it is not too late to change. Human beings are

marvelously adaptable, and the sex life of a couple can be renewed even after years of frustration. They must be willing, however, to try to accept each other and their respective needs for a sexual relationship. Happy is the woman who can rejoice that she is married to a man and can meet him freely. And happy is the husband who can awaken and cherish the love of his wife freely and un-apologetically. Their relationship will be one of mutual renewal, a point of focus for every other interest and aspect of it.

Where there has been difficulty, it may take time for a couple to rebuild the expression of their love. Each will have to accept the other's difficulties, fears, and stumbling efforts to overcome past patterns.

The Third Principle: *As partners in a sexual relationship, we must assume positive responsibility for that relationship.* Each must hold and express his sexuality for the other. The woman will not just hold whatever sexual life and desire she has passively as if it were a matter of indifference or dread to her if her husband approaches her. Instead, she may live it affirmatively by offering herself to him. She may show him that it is her pleasure, or that she wants it to be her pleasure to receive him, to be possessed by him. She may show him that she needs him or wants to need him. In these ways, among others, she may reveal her love for her husband.

So, likewise, the husband may give himself to his wife. He will try to take the man's part simply and confidently. He will try to act as though she wants him and will, there-fore, be better able to approach her with less anxiety and with more confidence. A woman wants a man to be a man. A man gives himself to his wife by disciplining his sex drive and response to what is commonly her slower response, to her rhythms, and to her need of wooing before, and companionship after, the act of love. Among others, these are ways in which he will exercise his sexual responsibility for her. This will mean self-denial and patience on the part of each, especially during the time that they are reworking their relationship. There will be times when they will have to accept disappointment as a part of the process of becoming accessible to each other, and will have to exercise gentleness and give encouragement.

Responsibility can also be exercised by reading some helpful books on marriage and, particularly, on sex relations. By reading and discussing what they read, a couple may help themselves to a more objective view. They may also acquire knowledge and insight that might help them to improve the quality and effectiveness of their sex life.

Responsibility can also be expressed by helping each other avoid the anxieties of achievement. For one thing, each couple ought to have intercourse as frequently as their age, health, and circumstances permit, without worrying as to whether they are having it as often as they should. Many people are afraid of not being "normal" in this respect. There is no universal norm; there is only that which is normal for each couple. Each partner may help the other to refrain from excessive performance for the sake of some expectation or standard, and to avoid unduly long periods of inactivity because of inertia or a drifting pattern of irresponsible inaction.

The Fourth Principle: *We must enter the sex relationships with the expectation that in the gift of each to the other we shall experience the power of renewal and reunion.* This does not mean that each attempt at love making will be an erotic success since there will be times when the attempted relationship will not come off in the way in which we should like. But even when it does not, there can still be the sense of intimacy, union, and love experienced because love and consideration are given.

For instance, many couples are concerned about simultaneous orgasm, which, in so much teaching and literature, is held up as the ideal achievement. Many people pursue this aim so anxiously that they both fail to enjoy their time together and fail to achieve the kind of climax they may have been led to believe they should have. The anxiety about this goal can become so severe that couples do not enjoy being together and sometimes reach the point where they can no longer even be together.

Simultaneous orgasm is not a possibility with each intercourse. Many women are capable of having and enjoying relations with their husbands without experiencing a climax every time. A more relaxed attitude toward the achievement of this goal will probably produce it more often than the anxious pursuit of it will; and, in addition, the couple will be able to enjoy and be fulfilled by their relationship together whether or not such a goal is achieved.

The sex relationship of a couple is like a trip to Seattle. There are two ways of going. It is conceivable that we might travel all the way at breakneck speed, looking neither to the right or left, and seeing nothing on the way—the "Seattle or bust" approach. If we arrive at all under these conditions, we are so nervously exhausted that there can be no sense of achievement. And this is the way some couples approach intercourse—a simultaneous orgasm-or-bust approach which often causes an anxiety-induced failure. A better way to go to Seattle is to take the time to enjoy the scenery along the way. If, for some reason, we do not get there, we have still enjoyed the trip. The chances are, however, that we shall arrive, and arrive more fulfillingly, just because we enjoyed the trip. And so a man and wife may come together in the love act, to love each other without compulsive objectives, and be renewed by that love, no matter what its experience may be.

By paying attention to each other, by accepting one another's nature, need, and potentiality, and by assuming responsibility for the other's experience in the relationship, the sex life of a couple may become a source of renewal and reunion to them. And they may undertake it with great expectations of love and healing.

In the novel *Sayonara* there is a description of a Japanese tea ceremony. After watching the stately and carefully executed ritual, an American turns to his Japanese companion and asks: "How come he makes a program out of everything?" She replies very simply, "The pleasure does not lie in the end itself; the pleasure lies in proceeding to that end." And so it is in the sexual, as in every other, relationship: The rewards lie in living, not in measuring our achievements.

In conclusion, we may say that sex does not need to be a problem and is not a curse as many conclude. Sex is a part of us all and is to be accepted as such. Since each person, male and female, is a unity of both physical and spiritual life, our real task is not to eradicate sex from our lives but direct it. We believe that apart from a fully committed relationship, sex relations can only result in exploitation and separation. Sexual desire is not evil as desire, but it is evil when we ignore the other person and his welfare because of that desire. If I use another's sexual function but by-pass him as a person, I am exploiting him. The evil of promiscuity is that it is an act against the person whose sexual function is thus exploited and becomes a sexual thing.

And, being an act against the person, it is also an act against the sanctity of all relationships of which the person is a part.

A holy sexual relationship is one in which the interrelatedness and wholeness of the person and his function is preserved and honored in thought and act. In holy love, the lover loves, honors, and cherishes his beloved as a person. It is a wonderful experience to be so revered as a person. And, in gratitude, the beloved gives her lover her functions as a thank-offering, even as he gives her his, so that the receiving is a result of giving in which there is a minimum of exploitation. In this sense, the sexual act is sacramental, for the act is an outward and visible sign of mutual union between two persons in which function serves its real purpose—to be an instrument for the realization of the fullness of the love relationship.

6

Five Ways to Creative Marriage

"We don't have time for each other any more. The business of living—children, work, church, and civic activities—stand between us. Not that it would make any difference if they didn't. We're probably grateful to these things for keeping us from having to face the truth of our situation . . .

"I wish I could step up on the porch, say, 'Julie!'—have her look at me and see me; and that in speaking her name, I could really see her again. . . . Things haven't been easy for her. I've hurt her. And there's a lot in her that's been stifled. Wish I could help, but I guess I'm the cause of her trouble."

—Dick Foster

6 The middle years of our life are the "some day" to which we looked when we started out as married couples very much in love. "Some day" was the time when our hopes and dreams would come true, even though we could not imagine being any more in love than we were, or being any happier. Still, something prompted us to look forward to a time when all this happiness of ours would bear fruit. Of course, that "some day" began immediately. We lived it as much during the first month of marriage as in the fifteenth year. Each moment and each year was the life that our love had persuaded us we wanted to live together. How has it been?

Some of us have spent the years with a sense of blessing. Of course, there were the betrayals, misunderstandings, disappointments, compromises, and despairs that two human beings experience when they try to express their love for each other and establish the intimate community of marriage and family. But mixed in with these experiences were the more dominant and memorable experiences of forgiveness, restored trust, strange peace, union and reunion, and other heroic achievements of our commitments to each other. We have learned that there cannot be joy without sadness, nor a sense of union without that desperate sense of being far away from each other. So our answer to the question, "How has it been?" is, "It's been good, profoundly good."

Others of us, however, do not recognize "some day" in today, and we do not look for it to come at all, now. "Nothing can be done to save our marriage," they say. "We can't start over again. We've made our mistakes and we are stuck with them. Now we have to make the best of it or quit."

Both groups have had, in one way, the same experience—that is, both have known the difficulties of living together. But, those of the first group have passed through these to the achievement of a happy marriage; the others have become stuck in the mire of human frustrations and resentment. Some of us have survived because we have been prepared to accept our humanity which not only inevitably complicates relationships but also makes them wonderful, as well. Others of us have had illusions about ourselves and others. We have been unprepared for our effect upon others and for their effect upon us.

We find ourselves married "for better, for worse," and the patterns of conjugal living made rigid by our years together. Our question may be: Are there no creative possibilities for us when we have failed to realize some of the promise of our relationship?

i

In the light of what we have said about love and sex, we now make some affirmations which may help in restoring to us the creative power of our marriages. These affirmations can help everyone, for no marriage is so good that it cannot be better, and no marriage is so bad that it cannot be improved. Every relationship can be opened to the possibility of growth because there is in each a potentiality for growth.

Our first affirmation is directed at the boredom which characterizes many marriages. Something can happen to our view of ourselves so that we no longer live with each other expectantly. Why should anyone expect anything of us if we live and think in sterile, formal ways? If we have become dull, we will naturally seem dull to others and perhaps to ourselves. We can fall into ruts of thought and action that are so deep we never escape them. Our partners can be misled by our robot-like existence into thinking that we are altogether predictable. Marriage should be stable and dependable, of course; novelty and excitement can be exhausting and a poor foundation for a relationship. On the other hand, a marriage cannot thrive when the partners as persons have curled up and turned yellow around the edges.

The affirmation against boredom is: *Since we are made in the image of God, there is more to each of us than the other sees.* There are depths and possibilities in each one of us that have never been plumbed or realized. Marriage is a relationship in which man and woman seek to reveal themselves and be known to one another. We must cling to a belief in the possibilities of a person. When we lose this sense of possibility of a person, we lose the possibility of a creative relationship with him. For instance, if a teacher assumes that his student can do only so much and is capable of only a certain kind of work and insight, his assumption may limit the pupil's power of achievement. But a teacher who has belief in a pupil may call forth responses that will be surprising to both. So, likewise in marriage, we should look for and encourage in each other the new untapped powers and unawakened interests.

Not only should we guard against expecting too little, but also against expecting too much. Julie Foster, as you may remember, was defeated by Dick's excessive demands of her. We all need the security of an accepting relationship. But we also need the stimulation of an expectant one. We need to believe in others and we need others to believe in us. This mutual respect and reverence for one another as persons is the source of our creative potentiality. The loss of reverence for what each of us is meant to be, destroys us and our relationships.

Some people fail to carry their worship of God over into

reverence for all that He made, including man. The work-man is to be honored in his work. Even though his work is less than he is, it bears his mark and expresses his image, and it is worthy of honor. On the contrary, our attitudes toward one another show that we have little honor for man, or for God, whose creation man is. But, when we look at each other through the love and mystery of God, we may begin to respect each other more and to see what we failed to see before: the possibilities in us of love and achievement even though these be obscured at the moment by our hostilities and failures. No matter how well we know an-other, there is always much more to be known.

How easily we type our partners and imprison them in stereotyped expectations. "Oh, him!" said a wife derisively when she was asked if her husband could do something. By the very tone of voice with which she uttered those two words, she pigeonholed him as an incompetent dud. Actually, however, he was an alert, capable person. We should avoid rigidly fixed expectations as mortal enemies since our relationships depend upon the creative expecta-tions of others. We must search for and encourage the unex-pressed love and capacity for living in ourselves and others. We must try to understand instead of judging. We must swing wide the gates of our expectations and, thereby, help our wives, husbands, children, and others to come into their creative heritage.

Our second affirmation in respect to marriage follows from what has just been said: *You will find your life by giving yourself and cherishing the other person.* In other words, the purpose of marriage is to call one another into being. Or, to put it another way, our business is to so live that we will help our partners to live.

An illustration of this principle appeared as Dick and

Julie Foster began to work out the difficulties of their relationship. It seemed that all his life he had a conception of what he thought Julie wanted him to be. He felt he had to match the picture of her conception of a good husband. And yet, all during their married life, he realized that he could never fit that picture. He wondered if she would love him unless he did meet her standards. As a result of living with these fears and attitudes, he became discouraged and tried to protect himself by immersing himself in his business. He thought that he had to become Julie's husband all by himself, independently of any assistance from her, and that only if he succeeded, would she love him. He felt that love had to be earned rather than its being a free gift.

On her side, Julie had suffered from Dick's anxiety about being a husband. She had wanted to help him, but had not known how to go about it. She had not been sure until lately what the difficulty was. His attitude produced in her a sense of helplessness which made it increasingly difficult for her to give him her love.

All during these years, Dick and Julie needed the help of the affirmation which we are now discussing: Our job as a person is to call one another into being. Dick did not have to become a husband by himself. He should have depended upon Julie to help him become her husband, even as she needed him to help her become a wife. If we stop to think about it, we know how true this is. A man discovers his masculinity as he lives in relation to a woman, and a woman her femininity as she lives in relation to a man. Here again we see how each calls the other into being. This is the way it was meant to be.

This is true of every relationship. The teacher has a responsibility to call his student into being, a parent his child. None of us is meant to live in isolation. None of us is meant to assume his respective responsibility by himself.

There is no such thing as a self-made man, for every man and every woman is dependent upon others for what they are and may become. The most that one can say is that this or that individual has made a maximum use of his own personal resources in relation to the aid that has come to him from others.

As we have seen before, this is the design of God for life. He created us to live in relation to one another and he set us in the midst of people. He intended that the meaning of our life should come from our association with one another, and that our vocation as persons is to call one another into life and being.

The basis of this is to be seen in the nature of God. All through the Bible we read that God is One who will not break that which is bruised, nor will He extinguish any good thing that burns even feebly. Instead "he gives power to the faint and to him who has no power he increases strength." The assurances are that they "who wait on the Lord will renew their strength." He forgives sin and heals infirmities. He saves life from destruction and gives mercy and loving kindness, and He fills the hungry with good things.

Here is the pattern for living together. We need to take inventory of our relationships and see what we are doing through them. What is our effect upon other men? Do we reject them and make their lot harder? Do we leave them alone in isolation to work out their responsibilities? Or, do we speak the word of love and encouragement? Do we live with them in ways that help them to feel the strength of our concern for them and the strength of our presence beside them so that they are better able to meet the demands and responsibilities of life?

More specifically, are we helping the women to whom we are married to be wives? Or do we merely make demands of them? If we only demand that they be what we want, they will fail because the burden of our demands will discourage them. They will fail for want of our love and the help it would be to them in being our wives. Are we helping the men to whom we are married to be husbands? They want to be, but they cannot do it by themselves. The power *to be* comes from God, but He wants us to be the instruments of this power for one another.

This business of calling one another into being means that the relationship of marriage, like any relationship, is a dialogue. In carrying on this dialogue, we must give ourselves and reveal ourselves as persons. This is the way the meaningful dialogue of relationship is begun. What we offer of ourselves may determine the response of the other person. If we offer a fake version of ourselves, we will probably get a fake return. But if we offer a real part of ourselves, we may get a real return. However, we cannot count on it. We may offer something real to another person and he may be so unsure of himself because of past experiences that he will not respond genuinely. Rather than withdraw when this occurs, we should face the real challenge of the vocation to call one another into being. If we turn and run because the offering of ourselves has not been appreciated or received in the way in which we meant it to be, we shall have failed. But if, with real courage, we let our offering stand, and stay with it, it may be that in time the other person will begin to trust and the real dialogue will at last begin. A heroic example of a courageous calling of a fearful and suspicious person into being was shown in the case of the artist George Duncan and Jane in Chapter 4.

In every marriage we must choose again and again whether we will offer each other a fake or a real self. For instance, we offer a fake self when we try to judge what is the expedient or wise thing to say in a given moment. We reach for an answer that will not cause trouble. We try to protect our partners by not saying the thing that perhaps we would like to say. We may go through a whole life together, weighing carefully each word to make sure that it is a word that will not disturb this relationship. What happens when we try to achieve peace in this fashion? It becomes increasingly impossible to find a word to speak. There follows long matrimonial silences that go on for years and years. It doesn't mean that the partners do not talk. It just means that they do not say anything. Or, it may mean that there is a great deal of verbal activity which is an attempt to cover up the silence or the meaninglessness. Partners to such a relationship do not feel that it is really safe to say anything. As the years pass, it becomes increasingly unsafe and increasingly impossible.

In contrast, there is the offering of the real self which calls forth the other. Mutual communication and revelation may now take place. It is much better to say what we mean even if the truth is disturbing. It would be much better to have a disturbance over a real revelation of ourselves to another than it would be to have a false kind of peace in which the sense of belonging to each other becomes impossible. Mutual revelation is the answer to deception. After all, we are driven to deceive one another because we are afraid our partners cannot take the truth about ourselves. We present ourselves to others, not as we really are, but as we think that person would like us to be. Our partners may put on their masks, too. Then we have the tragic situation of two persons behind their respective masks, trying to find each other. Only persons can relate, masks cannot. So if a husband and wife choose to wear masks, each will remain lost, alone, and—though married —unmarried.

Why choose such a hell of loneliness? The choice is between the pain that may accompany the revelation of ourselves and the hell of living alone. Why not choose the small bit of hell involved in revealing ourselves so we may cherish our mates? Then they can reveal themselves and be able to cherish us.

Marriage is like living in a house with windows. Windows let in the light. Occasionally we must wash the windows in order that the sunshine may shine in. Likewise in marriage, we have to wash the windows, both inside and out, so that we can see each other, find each other, talk to each other, live for each other, and in the end, love each other. When we are willing to do that, then the relationship is renewed. Each partner is then faithful to his vocation to call the other into being. Each cherishes and each is cherished.

Our third affirmation grows out of our recognition of differences: *The differences between man and woman can be good.* On several occasions thus far we have commented on these differences. Now the suggestion is that we accept and rejoice in the differences rather than fear them. Sometimes we hear young people boast that they have no differences: "We like the same things," they say, "nor do we have any disagreements." This condition is probably not as true as they want to think. If it were, they would sooner or later have a dull time together.

Many of us are afraid that the differences will have an injurious effect upon our marriage. We may try to obliterate them or to pretend that they aren't there. We move toward false and premature similarities in an attempt to cover them over. We may pretend to like the same things for the sake of a superficial agreement. We can only do this at the cost of some interest or taste that is important to us. The surrender of them for the sake of unanimity in a relationship may provoke hostility rather than nurture love. Couples have been known to live together for years under the illusion that they were "perfectly" mated and enjoyed all the same things although all the while they were doing inconsiderate and even cruel things to each other which probably expressed their resentment of the frustration and monotony of their marriage.

My suggestion is, therefore, that we rejoice in our differences, bring them out, look at them, talk about them, examine them, wear them one way one time, another way the next time.

There are two kinds of differences between married partners. There are the first and obvious sex differences: the physical, emotional, and mental differences between men and women which are necessary to marriage and which may be the occasion either for division or for a complementary enrichment of the relationship.

On the other hand, there are the differences between the partners as persons. It may have nothing whatever to do with their sexual difference. The effect of these differences, too, can be divisive or enriching.

One of the most dramatic personality differences existed in a couple who had been married for at least twenty-five years. The woman was years older than her husband. She was much interested in art, literature, and the aesthetic side of life. He was interested in mechanical things, hunting, fishing, outdoor life. While she read a great deal, he had not opened a book since he left high school. She was responsive to ideas, and he was responsive to things. They were so completely opposite that if any of us had been asked to prejudge their marriage, we would have said it could not possibly have succeeded. Actually, they had achieved a rich relationship full of mutual respect and interest. They enjoyed living separately in their respective interests, and in their life together their devotion to each other was a revelation to see. The achievement of their marriage was not easy because they had had difficulties. Each had made sacrifices in the interests of the other and of their life together. The richness of their marriage was due to the acceptance, rather than the obliteration, of their differences. Nor did they pretend that differences did not exist. Each listened to the other, and each learned to be interested in the other's interests. Each learned to respond and to participate to a certain extent. Since they were able to do this, each was much richer for the difference which the other brought to the relationship. Their life taught the great lesson—*let differences complement each other*. Their example encourages us to see the positive rather than the negative side of differences. And although it takes courage to live affirmatively with differences, it can be done!

ii

Our thoughts about differences between us lead us to our fourth affirmation which deals with the much publicized condition of incompatibility: *Compatibility is the achievement of marriage, not a condition necessary to its beginning.* We should not be surprised that compatibility between persons is not ready-made and is harder to achieve than is at first thought. After all, our Christian doctrine of man teaches us that we are not only self-centered but selfish as well. As the late Archbishop Temple wrote, "Some things hurt us; we hope they will not happen again; we call them bad. Some things please us; we hope they will happen again; we call them good. Our standard of values is the way things affect ourselves, so each of us takes his place in the center of his own world." This is what makes each of us fundamentally incompatible with the other. Inevitably, we compete and clash. Compatibility, then, is not a gift but an achievement. And every marriage has to take into account elements of incompatibility that are always lurking in the shadows.

The case of Eric and Janice illustrates the point. They had been going together for several years and were, as they put it, passionately in love. They were a storybook couple. He was tall, dark, and handsome; she small, attractive, feminine. I noticed that their feeling for each other was not only warm and deep, but also very intense. Eric, however, was an easy-going, relaxed person, not given to showing much his serious side; whereas Janice, for all of her occasional gay moods, seemed to take life much more seriously. Sometimes when they were together, it seemed as if they were both very anxious about their future marriage and were hiding from this anxiety. Janice's parents had been divorced, on grounds of incompatibility, after ten years of marriage. Separation and consequent loss of her father had been a shock to her. In the course of a conversation with a counselor, she said, with strong feeling, "Nothing like that must happen to Eric and me!"

Eric, with some exasperation, asked, "Why should it?"

"There is no reason, I guess," replied Janice, "except that I worry so about the possibility. We mean so much to each other it would be dreadful if anything should happen to change us."

Showing on his face his increasing exasperation and anxiety, although visibly trying to control himself, Eric finally burst out, "I really don't see what you are worrying about. Just because your Dad and Mom broke up doesn't mean that we have to! You worry too much. You are always borrowing trouble when you don't need to!"

Janice looked at Eric in amazement and retorted, "Eric, you can't mean what you are saying! If you do, what I have just said has already begun to come true! Maybe we are too different for our marriage to work. You're always laughing things off and making jokes of them. I haven't said anything, but you often hurt my feelings. Life is serious. You'd think so, too, if you'd been through the mess I have!"

Recovering somewhat and taking Janice's hand, Eric admitted, "We are different, Janice, but that ought to be good. I guess we will have some trouble because of it."

"That's it!" interrupted Janice. "I've had enough trouble, all because Mother and Dad were incompatible. I don't want to make the same mistake they did. O Eric, I love you, but I'm so afraid we will have trouble."

Eric and Janice were a normal young couple who fortunately were able to discover before their marriage that the differences between people are inevitable and can cause trouble even between two people who love each other. They also discovered that compatibility is not an inheritance which one receives at the beginning of a relationship. Now that they are married, they are discovering that it begins to appear as they live together. Even Janice was able to accept their uncongenialities and learned not to interpret them as signs that their relationship was failing. They took occasions of disagreement as a matter of course. Sometimes, because of their differences, they became estranged, but instead of saying their marriage was finished, they accepted the estrangement as something for their love to work on.

Our conclusion is simple. When trouble comes and we are hurt and estranged, and when it looks as if we are incompatible, we should learn to accept the situation as an invitation for more love rather than as an indication of the end of love. This is a way of living the affirmation: "Compatibility is the achievement of a marriage." If we can accept this as a normal part of life, we will be better prepared for all of life's experiences. We will not be put off and distracted by the unhappy parts, and we will be better able to love and realize its power in our lives.

The perfect portrayal of what I have been talking about is seen in Christ's love for us. His love accepted the incompatibilities between man and man and between man and God, and He overcame them. But look what happened in the process! There is the Cross and the Crucifixion. This part of the Gospel tells us that pain, suffering, surrendering of self, and the endurance of hostility must always be a part of a relationship in which love is at work. The Gospel also tells us that the triumph and the Resurrection, the restoration of relationship, is to be found on the other side of the Crucifixion and is not to be had without going through it. Here is the road for lovers of all kinds, whether the object of love is man or woman or a great cause. The road has its lovely and gentle stretches, but other parts are fearsome and demanding. In the end, if we stay on this road, we will come to a great place where all longing is fulfilled, all estrangements reunited, all brokenness mended and healed. When we let love lead us through all that life brings us, we find the full joy of loving and being loved.

The Christian story describes the love of God as a love which will not be put off by anything. The Parable of the Prodigal Son, for instance, could be called the Parable of the Astonishing Love of the Father. You remember how the father received his son. The boy was a beggar and a disgrace, but the father went out to meet him and treated him as though he were a great success and covered with glory, greeted him with honors, not because he was a success, but because he was his son.

The story is told of a Chinese artist who undertook to

paint this story. His first attempt showed the father standing, waiting at the gate for his son who was seen approaching in the distance. When the artist showed his picture to a Christian friend, his friend exclaimed, "Oh, no, you don't have it right. The father shouldn't be standing, waiting. He should be running to meet his son."

"But no Chinese father could do that!" said the artist.

"That is just the point," replied his friend. "No human father would, but this is the astonishing story of a father that tells us about God's amazing love—He loves us like that!"

"I see," replied the artist.

The next picture he painted showed the father running to meet his son, and, in his hurry, he had put on shoes that didn't match.

In this way, God's love overcomes our incompatibility, and it is this power of love, His and ours, working together that can overcome the differences that seem to make us uncongenial and threaten the destruction of our relationships upon which we depend.

Our fifth and final affirmation in respect to marriage is: *It takes time to be married.* You know the old song "Take Time to Be Holy." Well, take time to be married. It's one way of finding wholeness which is not unrelated to holiness. This affirmation is related to the modern situation which leaves little time for marriage. Father is so consumed by his work and so conscious of the little that he may be doing for his children, that his role as husband fills him with a sense of guilt. Mother is so overwhelmed in her attempt to be a woman in this confused culture and with trying to be a mother that she doesn't have much time and energy left for her role as wife.

We live in a day when it is popular for parents to give

everything to their children, to live for their children. Children, like the rest of us, respond by taking everything they can get. It isn't good for them to have all of our attention, nor is it good for us to give it. Our children need a relationship with parents who continue to be husband and wife, because we cannot be good parents unless we are also husbands and wives. We should not give them all our time, energy, and love. The time we take away from our children and from other responsibilities and interests to devote to each other furnishes us with the opportunity to work through our difficulties and build our relationship. Our children will profit from our taking time to be married because they are more likely then to have happy and helpful parents.

Children need us to be persons, to be men and women, and, therefore, husbands and wives. As they live with us and observe our living together as men and women, as husbands and wives, they themselves are helped to become men and women to assume the role of husband and wife, and, eventually, of parent to their own children. We need to take time to be married in order that our children may have an opportunity to see how husbands and wives may live together in a relationship of mutual love and encouragement and deal with the tensions and problems of marriage and family.

We ought to take time to be married because our children will eventually leave us to live their own lives, and we shall then, after they are gone, have to resume our husband-wife relationship. They are with us only a brief time, and our marriage will last longer than the period of our children's dependency. Most marriages fall into a pattern like this: One or two years as a couple before the children come; then twenty to thirty years or more during which we build our homes, bear and rear our children, and establish ourselves in our work and community life; finally, the children leave and husband and wife find themselves alone again. If, during our busy middle years, we do not take time to be married, we may find that we have no marriage left. Children come and go, but we husbands and wives are meant to go on together, dependent upon one another for love and strength. We need to build for our future as well as for the children's. We can build an enduring community of interest by learning to do things together and by developing independent interests and activities. If we do not take pains to build our own lives, we will have nothing to draw us together. Unless we take time to be married, we will have no marriage for the rest of the time.

The counsel here is that, while we are younger and in the midst of raising our families, we need to take thought and prepare for the time when we shall be alone. We were important to each other before the children came. We are important to each other for the sake of the children. And we shall be important to each other after the children are gone. If we have already made the mistake of not building for the time when we will be alone again, it is not too late to rebuild.

Some may say, "This is all very well, but the advice, sound as it is, comes too late. We have neglected each other and now we are as strangers, and as strangers we must remain." No! Here again is another underestimation of the human spirit, of the power of love as it works in and between people. If we think that creative changes cannot occur, they will not; but if we are aware of the possibilities of achieving a new point of view and way of life, we shall achieve them more easily.

Even now we can take time to rediscover each other, to find new interests and things to do, together or separately, such as hobbies, services to the community, study projects, and the like.

Not only children but a man's work can steal time from his marriage and family. The demands of modern business and professional life make ruthless claims on men today— make them not only on men but on their wives as well. One young man reported that it was necessary for him to spend 450 extra hours a year on his job. Many professional men devote from 500 to 1000 hours a year additional to the normal working day in an attempt to increase their practice or to maintain it once it has been established. Men cannot work like that and still have time, energy, or interest left over for their families. And whatever effort they make is more likely to be devoted to the children with the result that their relationships with their wives get the short end of the deal. It is no wonder that they discover in later years that they are strangers and have nothing in common.

In short, we need to save time from every demand and responsibility to give to nurturing the growth of our marriages. Every responsibility of family, work, and community will be met more creatively if the partners of a marriage are able to live out of the renewal that comes from conjugal fulfillment.

Marriage is a school, a great school of the person. No other personal relationship calls for the same depth and constancy of commitment. In what other is a man and woman so unqualifiedly confronted by the truth of himself in relation to others? In what other relationship are the possibilities for repentance and forgiveness any greater? In what other relationship is it possible to find the resources of love to live creatively with disillusionment and heart-break? Or where else in human relations is there to be found such depth of joy? Nowhere else is there such exciting dialogue between love and hate. Although marriage is a very human institution, it is a means of grace: that is, a means of help which comes ultimately from the Source of all love —God Himself.

CHAPTER 7

For Parents of Adolescents

"It's hard to think straight about our family, we seem so messed up. Wonder if others are like us?

"Julie and I tried to help Bernard and Jane. There's sure a big gap between wanting to do something and doing it. Something gets into kids in their adolescence that makes them harder to understand and to handle. Bernard was defiant, as if he were trying to prove something. It was as if he had a chip on his shoulder and dared me to knock it off. I couldn't figure out whether he was making a bid for more discipline or whether I wasn't giving him enough freedom . . . I failed him as a father without knowing why. He had a way of making me awfully mad. It's funny how the feeling of helplessness makes you angry. Then I'd feel guilty about it all. We lost touch with each other during his teens. Something came between us. I've often wished we could get it out in the open and talk about it. Now lately things seem a little better . . .

"With Jane it was different. She was such an eager little thing and she obviously wanted to please everybody, especially her mother. They were very close when she was little. When she reached her teens, the strains began. Yet after she had been defiant about something, she was very repentant and couldn't do enough to show how sorry she was. She could never stand quarrels. Sometimes they really made her sick. She was always a peacemaker, and she worked hard for approval. She was almost too cooperative. Julie worried about Jane because she was too good. She felt that Jane did not look out for her own interests enough. I couldn't see anything wrong with her, but something must have been wrong. We gave her everything, including love. That's supposed to be enough . . . but it didn't seem to be."

—Dick Foster

7 We now come to the important —even if sometimes satisfying, sometimes baffling—responsibility of people in their middle years, the responsibility of parenthood. Despite our having been parents for many years, many of us are now having new, and often disturbing, experiences with our youngsters, which are causing us to question how effective our parental role has been. We have strong fellow feelings for Dick and Julie Foster. If we could speak with them, we would readily assure them that they are not alone since we too share with them anxieties and feelings of guilt. For it is not hard to be gloomy about the bad effects we may be having upon the development of our children. Our mistakes seem so obvious to us. Even parents who, on the whole, are having a happy time with their children have these same misgivings. With Dick we say that we love our children, but we wonder if that love is good enough. There are times when we feel sorry both for our children and for ourselves. This reaction of self pity is not, of course, creative, although very human and understandable.

The parental situation is complex—indeed, frighteningly so. It is easy for us to see where things have gone wrong, but not always so easy to see what we ought to do. It is easy to feel guilty when we are guilty, but it is very much harder for us to feel confident about our attempts to do something constructive. The purpose of this chapter is to help parents face, with courage and confidence, their parental responsibility to children who have reached some degree of maturity and who, because of their maturity, are not so easily understood or so readily open to care and guidance as they were when younger.

Sometimes our discussion of these problems may seem to

make the handling of human situations too easy. It should be remembered that it is always easier to talk or write about life than it is to live it. There are two dangers, therefore, that we must try to avoid. On the one hand, we can be misled by oversimplifying the problems; on the other, we can make situations that are relatively simple unnecessarily complex. Furthermore because much that we deal with is concerned with problems—problems that worry or confuse us—we should not conclude that life with young people consists of problems only. For the truth is adolescents are exciting, companionable, mysterious, lovable and loving, and they move through their days with all the speed, thrill, and ups-and-downs of a roller coaster.

i

The problems arising from the parent-adolescent relationship are twofold: those of the growing adolescent, and those of parents. We shall consider the adolescent's problems first.

Previously, in Chapter 2, we observed how adolescents withdraw from the close, intimate, confidential relationship that they had with their parents earlier. We also saw how their nurture during infancy and childhood brings them to a point where they are able to dare this withdrawal in order to become persons in their own right with responsibility for themselves. Thus, they make the transition from the state of life in which they need to be loved to one in which they need to love and are able to do so. We saw further that during this period, adolescents have three principal tasks to accomplish: first, the task of liberation from their old attachments and the achievement of self-reliance and self-direction. Second, the task of deciding what they are going to do with their lives, including the choice (if they have a choice) of how they will make their living. Third, the task of completing their sexual development and of becoming heterosexual adults whose primary interest is in the opposite sex. This final stage of development, in most cases, ultimately leads them to choose a member of the opposite sex as a life-long partner. These three tasks are a tremendous undertaking for all adolescents. Opposed to the powers within themselves that help them to accomplish these tasks, there are resistances, resistances in themselves, in their families, and in the culture around them.

The resistances within themselves stem from a natural reluctance to leave the old familiar and secure relationships in which they have known security. Their feelings about growing up are mixed. They both want to break with the old and establish the new, but they also have a nostalgic longing for the old and familiar which they are reluctant to surrender. Their resistances to growing up stem also from a fear of the new life that is opening up to them, and a fear that they will not be able to employ the new powers which they are beginning to possess. They are in the grip of the same fear of the unknown as besets us even in our adult lives. Here again, adolescents' feelings are mixed. Although they want to use their powers, they are afraid of them. They want new responsibilities, yet the prospect frightens them. The unknown is both exciting and fearful. Their bizarre behavior is due partly to their efforts to overcome these resistances. Emotionally, they have to wrench themselves free from the old and with much bravado undertake the new, a process which may lead them, for instance, to proclaim arrogantly that they are fed up with their parents who, by the way, have never done right by them, have always stood in their way. They may also repudiate everything they have been taught and defiantly take a stand on religious or political issues opposed to that held by their parents, to the one in which they were nurtured.

Parents and other adults important to adolescents have their difficulties, too, in accepting youths' need and efforts to grow up. The achievement of maturity, however, cannot take place in a vacuum, but must be nourished and sustained by the relationships in which teenagers live. Yet because parents find it difficult to keep pace with the changes and developments in their children, they sometimes unwittingly resist and obstruct what their children have to think and feel and do in order to grow and develop.

During the recess of a conference on the difficulties between adolescents and parents, one mother was heard to say, "Thank God, my Bill has never had any of these difficulties. He loves me just as much as he ever did. He has never given me a moment of trouble, and has always done what I've wanted him to do." Of course, this mother did not know the true meaning of what she was saying. Instead of rejoicing over her son's behavior, she ought to have been alarmed and asking for help. Fortunately, many parents are not this blind, but it is still difficult for most of us to understand what is going on in the process of development, and sometimes it is very difficult for us not to get in the way of it.

Why do we parents resist these developments in our children's growth? In the first place, our awareness of what is going on in them does not keep pace with their actual development so that we are often unprepared for the changes that begin to occur. Suddenly we are forced to realize that our children are no longer "little children." They have grown up! They are asserting themselves and are quite capable of making and carrying out decisions, the maturity of which surprises us. Dick Foster was surprised by his son's request to be allowed to go off on a summer's expedition by himself. That our children are capable of doing this kind of thing is often hard to accept. The habit of paternalism in dealing with them is hard for us to break. If we resist too strenuously their efforts to emancipate themselves, they will, if they are mentally and physically healthy, make still other and more vigorous attempts to achieve their purpose. Their renewed effort to break the old ties and patterns may cause them to behave even more defiantly, and this further alarms us and stiffens our resistance to what they are trying to accomplish. Finally, both children and parents lose the whole point of the incident with the result that both are frustrated and resentful. But in these instances we have to remember that it is not easy for either an individual or a nation to declare their independence, and it often takes a revolution of some violence before that independence is achieved.

Moreover, in our resistance to the pattern of adolescent growth we sometimes find ourselves opposed not only to what they are trying to do, but also to how they are doing it. We do not mind a child's falling down when he is learning to walk, but we do object to his falling down when he is learning to live. Similarly, in response to their need to be grown up, adolescents often attempt an action that not only does not come off successfully but may even be an embarrassing fiasco for all concerned. This is like falling down while trying to learn to walk. Adolescents experience parental resistance in the reactions of their parents to any trouble arising from their efforts to grow up. There is no doubt that falling down is dangerous, dangerous not only for the individual but for his parents as well. But risk and danger are part of growing up and have to be accepted by both children and parents. Furthermore, if they are not made anxious about falling down, maybe adolescents will not fall down so often or so disastrously. In fact, it is the anxious adolescents who make the most errors of judgment and are driven by their inner compulsions to more dangerous escapades. Actually, the more serious danger is not that adolescents will make mistakes or disgrace themselves and their parents, but that they will not accomplish their tasks, that they will not grow up. This is the worst tragedy that can befall them, and the one we parents should dread more than the accidents which may happen in the process.

The achievement of independence does not necessarily mean the repudiation of the home as something undesirable, and of parents as a liability. Periods of rebellion and withdrawal are usually followed by periods of renewed and deepened relationship when the meaning of home to the adolescent receives a new and stronger affirmation. This transition is an indication that the youngsters have shaken themselves free from childish attachments and bonds and are now able to give themselves as responsible individuals to those upon whom they were formerly dependent. For they cannot successfully face life if they remain dependent upon their parents. And, as parents, we must be willing that they throw off both these dependencies; indeed, we must help them do so.

Our resistance to their growing up is clearly to be seen in the ways we react to their sexual development. When it first begins to appear that a boy and girl are interested in each other, we may either try to keep them apart because we are afraid of what might happen, or we may try to promote the relationship prematurely for fear that our child will not be popular. Or, at another time, we may try to select the boys or girls whom we want our adolescent to date. Or, we may show our resistance by ridiculing their new interest in one another and their efforts to learn to be together satisfyingly. Again, we may show our resistance by setting up false ideals for the relationship, such as telling a boy that he should treat his girl as if she were his mother—a ridiculous counsel for a boy who is both trying to overcome his dependence on his mother and achieve a relationship with the opposite sex. We also show our resistance by our being afraid that in the process of working out their hetero-sexual relationship, things will happen to our children. Of course, things will happen! They are meant to happen no matter what we do about them, and it is much better that they happen in the context of a relationship from which the young person can expect understanding and help. About this more will be said later.

The efforts of adolescents to achieve maturity plus the effects of the resistance they meet in themselves and others combine to produce great confusion for them. It is no wonder that they are mixed up and aimless; no wonder that we adults are perplexed by their behavior and by our relation to them. We are often misled by the degree of their physical growth and the occasional evidences of their maturity into thinking that they are more competent than they really are, and thus we fail to provide the direction and guidance they need. They are eager for whatever adult privileges they can get, but they are not so eager to accept the respon-sibilities that go with them. Young people are great seekers after pleasure but have strong aversions to work or to any-thing that limits or disciplines their desires.

Undoubtedly, young people are often the victims of the inconsistencies and confusions of the people around them. Some of the mismanagement and failure that they experi-ence at our hands is the cause of delinquency which, in turn, is a sign of their protest. But the chief concern of most of us is the ambiguity of our relationship with our young people. We wish that there were more confidence between them and us, and that, within reasonable limits, we were more success-ful in communicating with them and they with us.

·· ii

Let us turn now to a consideration of the parent's situation, whose concern and point of view is an equally important consideration. Sometimes the literature on adolescents seems to emphasize the needs and rights of the young at the expense of the needs and rights of parents. But parents are important, too. Actually, adolescents suffer when parents are not duly considered. And since adolescents are still dependent upon them, parents need to feel that their concerns are legitimate ones, that their point of view may be justifiable, and that they are also respected as persons. Therefore, it is important for us to examine the parents' situation.

In the first place, we parents are human. We, too, make mistakes of judgment in the exercise of our responsibilities and we sin against those whom we love. We recognize, as did Dick Foster, that there is a big gap between wanting to do the right thing and being able to do it. Being human means that we often find it hard to keep the main issue in focus. Being human means that we become emotionally entangled in the problems of our children, even when we try to avoid that. Being human also means that we are confused many times when faced with finding a balance between the exercise of our authority and the freedoms that we grant our youngster for the sake of their development. Being human means that it is hard to keep our love from becoming possessive and from trying to prevent our children from making the same mistakes we did. And it means that we will be anxious about the welfare of those for whom we are responsible.

On the other hand, being human can mean that we have a power of loving that is necessary to the well-being of others, and especially of our children. When we admit that we are human, we acknowledge that we have limitations; but we also confidently affirm that we have resources for fulfilling our parental role. We are much better parents when we are able to accept the fact that we are human, and thus do not unrealistically expect too much of our parental capacities. I have talked to many parents whose chief difficulty seemed to be that they were frantically and anxiously trying to be perfect. A perfect parent is an impossibility in view of our humanity. The sooner we give up illusions about ourselves and what we can accomplish, the more helpful we shall be, and the happier will our youngsters be. This does not mean that we will stop trying to fulfill our responsibilities, but that we will stop trying to do the impossible.

Second, the situation of parents is complicated because they are often made the scapegoat for others' failures. A scapegoat is one upon whom people symbolically place their sins in order to be rid of them. Sometimes ministers, doctors, teachers, social workers, and therapists of various kinds are tempted to point their fingers accusingly at parents for their failures, and heap upon them responsibility for the crises of adolescence. It has been a favorite indoor sport to make jest of the failures and ineptitudes of confused parents. Parents who are bowed down by their responsibilities and anxious about their failures are natural preys for the modern game of scapegoating. Confused by the task of being parents, it is not hard for them to be convinced that they are, indeed, a miserable lot who ought to know better.

Of course, parents have done their own scapegoating, too. It is not uncommon for them to blame the schools for what is happening to youngsters, and to complain about the church doing so little to help young people grow up in this confused and confusing age. And yet no one else has been made to feel the burden of the sins of our generation more than present-day parents. There is much injustice in these accusations, and parents should resist assuming responsibilities not rightly theirs. They should not assume reponsibilities that belong to others. It is bad enough for them to carry their own load of guilt, without carrying the guilt that belongs to others. One of the first constructive steps parents can take in this direction is to try to determine, and accept, their true responsibility, then to repudiate the responsibility that belongs to others.

Third, parents have been victims of radical changes in the philosophies and methods of raising children. Many of us were raised under the concept that the child was to be seen, not heard. The authority that we experienced was often imperious, if not tyrannical. Conformity to parental rule was required. Freedom was something we achieved after we left the parental home. Next, we either experienced as children, or were taught to practice as parents, the philosophy that children were not to be cuddled, but to be treated quite objectively. If they fell down, let them pick themselves up. If they cried, do not go to them and cuddle them. Feed them on schedule, be consistent and unsentimental. Next, we were taught the reverse: Give your children unlimited expressions of love, do not frustrate them in any way, give them free opportunity to express anything they want from love to hostility; and never deprive them of anything they want. The important thing was that every whim of theirs should be fulfilled so that they might know security. The theory was that once they had been made secure and had expressed their hostility, they would become mature and loving. Many of us, however, were dismayed to discover that we had only succeeded in establishing patterns for the expression of hostility. Far from becoming mature, they continued to look for infantile forms of security.

Now, the pendulum has swung a little more to the right, and we find ourselves being urged to show our love by being strong, by exercising authority, and by helping the individual to experience deprivations as a necessary part of life. These and other changes in the concepts of child care have made the situation unbelievably confusing for many conscientious parents. In fact, many of these changes have occurred so rapidly that some parents confess that each of their children was raised by a different philosophy. Many a family situation is a monument to the confusion, not of parents, but of the experts and philosophers. These students of human behavior are not to be blamed for the confusion, however; for they, too, are human. They uncover the truths about human nature in separate pieces and discover its meaning in relation to other insights only dimly and gradually. Furthermore, there is no point in placing blame whether on parents, teachers, or researchers. The more creative approach is to accept our human situation; and each of us, with whatever resources we have, try to meet it constructively.

The fourth characteristic of the parental situation is that children, as they grow older, become more difficult to live with and care for. In their earlier years, they are easier to understand and "manage." There is a good deal more known about infants and children than about adolescents, and the knowledge has been more available to parents in printed form. Then, too, young children are more accessible as persons in that they usually tell their parents everything. They have no problems about being dependent although there is a growing desire and capacity to be independent which they express, for example, by saying, "Let me do it!

Let me do it!" But, for the most part, they want, need, and accept parental care and decision. So characteristic is this that when they begin to repudiate this kind of parental relationship, parents may be shocked by it.

Adolescents, in contrast to what they were earlier, become strange and unmanageable from the parents' point of view. They withdraw from the old confidential kind of relationship, become self-conscious, and mysterious. We no longer know what they are thinking or what they are going to do. More than ever they want to be a law unto themselves, keep their own counsel, suffer in silence, and begin to share with us and all adults the separation of existence.

This means, of course, that our relationship with them is changing, and the changing relationship means that the old methods of living with them are no longer adequate. Since they do not tell us what their troubles are and we do not have any way of knowing what they are, we cannot step in and straighten things out for them. Indeed, any attempt to do so is interpreted by them as interference. What we might offer as intervention will be regarded by them as interference. One of their constant complaints is, "Why do you treat me like a baby?" Often their complaint is a just one. Our actions do violence to their sense of being and take away from them a sense of dignity which they are newly acquiring with such great difficulty.

If the old methods are inadequate for the new relationship, it is obvious that our task is to try to evolve new ways of living with these changing individuals. Yet this is not easy to do. In the first place, they are anything but stable at this age. Many people are unprepared for the ups and downs of human development. They mistakenly assume that our growth and maturity proceeds with regular progression. Actually the movement is more a forward-and-backward one. At one time our teenagers can be very mature and we can rejoice in the progress they are making. But the next day they can slip back to a distressing degree of childishness. At such times we may become discouraged with them and feel that they will never grow up. So, back and forth between maturity and immaturity growing individuals move, and they need parents and teachers who can move with them. When they are being more mature, they want and need a mature response from their parents. When they are being immature, they still want to be respected as persons; but they need the kind of acceptance that will help them grow.

With great exasperation an adolescent exclaimed to his mother, "Believe me I'm not going to raise my kids the way I was. I'm going to have discipline in my house, and there won't be any arguing." Out of momentary feelings of immaturity and confusion, he grasps for security and indicates his need for a firm and guiding hand.

Needless to say, this places great responsibility upon parents and teachers, and explains why so many people become so exasperated with adolescents. But it seems to help parents in being more accepting and helpful to know that this is the nature of adolescence.

Fifth, another aspect of the parent situation is that when we are baffled by the job of being parents of adolescents, we may make our children scapegoats for our own feelings of guilt and anxiety. In other words, we may be tempted to take our feelings of frustrations and helplessness out on teenagers. This is not good mental hygiene for us, and it certainly adds a bewildering burden on them. They have enough troubles without taking on ours, especially when they are unable to understand the effect they produce in us. It is hard for them to really believe the despair they can create in us. When we therefore make scapegoats out of them for our own feelings, they do not know what it is all about. Sometimes it is helpful to both of us for us to explain to them what it means to be a parent. The relationship between us can be a part of the curriculum of living from which they can learn some necessary lessons that will prepare them for their own responsibilities. Here, again, we need to avoid the method we used when they were children, namely the method of protecting them from anything that would disrupt their sense of security. Now, they need to deal with some of the real problems and issues of life. With the help of parents and teachers, they can be guided and instructed in the handling of them. This will undoubtedly provoke anxiety, but anxiety is a part of life; and, in this instance, learning to live with it is a part of the curriculum of the school of life. Adolescents need relationships with parents and teachers within which, and by the help of which, they can experience and learn to deal with anxiety.

It is true, however, that our own anxieties as parents and teachers are activated by the anxieties of our young people. For instance, parents who have some anxieties about their own social standing are likely to have some difficulty in helping a teen-age girl with her popularity problems. In such a case, it is better for the mother to share with her daughter their mutual concerns about social life, than to pretend that no such problem exists and yet to be so emotionally involved in trying to help the daughter that the daughter's situation is made worse. For in this latter situation what the mother is really doing is trying to work out her own problem through her daughter's life rather than honestly facing with her daughter a common human problem.

Sixth, another typical parental situation is that where parents have difficulty in accepting the fact that human beings fail and make mistakes. As teenagers face such problems as their relationship with the opposite sex, they become involved in all kinds of relationships with one another in which they experiment, test their standards, exercise whatever powers of self-discipline and responsibility they have, and in the process, both succeed and fail. Some things they do will be good; others will be unfortunate and even tragic. No one in his right mind would underestimate the seriousness of things that can happen to young people as a result of their trying to find their way to maturity. But as we said before, nothing is more important than their arriving at that point of maturity where they are capable of living responsibly in relation with others. Since this is true, they need parents and teachers who can pass through these various experiences with them, help and guide them, and, in general, provide a relationship in which they will be better able to deal with whatever happens. Being able to deal creatively with whatever happens is one of the greatest tests of a parental or teaching relationship.

A father faced this challenge when his son, because of anger toward him, drove off in a great rush and wrecked the family car. After the first emotional reaction had passed, the father remembered that, serious as the boy's action was, their relationship to one another was more important. In order to help his son with the real issue, namely his feelings toward him, he had to accept the wrecked car as only a symptom of what was wrong and not as the main point. In the end, the growth of the relationship between father and son put the issue of the wrecked car in right perspective. In times of crisis, there is a great temptation to see relationships and situations out of focus. If we act out of this false focus, we can seriously impair our relationship which is the only resource we have to deal with the real trouble. It is not hard to be a parent when things go well: the real test is when things do not go well, and our children get into trouble. This is one of the lessons that Dick and Julie Foster are learning from their counselor about their relations with their children. They are beginning to see that Bernard and Jane's difficulties are not nearly so serious when they, Julie and Dick, can bring an accepting and undefensive relationship to the situation. Although Jane's illness has seriously dislocated her life, at least for the time being, what she chiefly needs at present are parents and friends who can accept what has happened as part of her life and who can add their resources to hers for facing the situation. This is what the artist, George Duncan, did and this is what she needs from everyone. Her responses will be much more creative in this kind of relationship than in any other.

The same principle is relevant to Dick and Julie's relationship to each other. It is unfortunate, even tragic, that they became as separated from one another as they did. There is no point in trying to fix blame for it. The important thing is for them to accept and deal with their relationship and to try to learn from it those lessons that may eventually deepen it.

Finally, parents have to accept the fact that heredity, as well as environment, influences the course of events for good or ill. We have had a period of thinking that every thing was determined by the environment in which people lived. The pendulum is beginning to swing back and give some importance to heredity. One of the best illustrations of the influence of heredity is the differences that exist between children in the same family. One child responds to the family situation in one way; another child in another.

Sometimes parents want their sons and daughters to be like them. It may be hard for a mother to discover that the daughter is like the father, or the father to discover that the son is like the mother. Or, both may be dismayed to discover that their children are more like some other member of their family. This effect of heredity is seen not only in physical appearance, but in personality traits as well. As parents we have to be prepared for these individual differences that stem from the genes. Or we may be troubled because our children do not make as good use of their opportunities as we think they should. We like to think that if the environmental resources were better and our children worked harder, the desired results would come. The source of the difficulty may not be in the environment but in the hereditary possibilities.

This, of course, raises the question of the relationship between heredity and environment which has been debated by philosophers and scientists through the centuries. Needless to say, this book does not undertake to settle the matter, but I have found the following principles to be of help. Heredity sets limits and determines the character within which the development of the individual may take place. Environmental influences determine how far within those limits the individual may develop. The counsel here is that we use the resources of environment as creatively as possible in order that our youngsters may achieve as much as possible within the limits of their endowment. However, while doing this, we need to remember that their response to these resources is also partly determined by their inheritance. We may have to accept that what any given adolescent is or does is determined as much by his heredity as by environmental influences, including our own influence. The converging of hereditary and environmental influences on an individual presents us with a mystery before which we must sometimes only bow reverently without being able to see and understand exactly what is going on.

. . .
iii

We turn now to a consideration of some suggestions that may help us meet our responsibilities as parents more creatively. Immediately we need to remind ourselves that parenthood is one of the major relationships of life, along with the relationship between husband and wife. We need, further, to remind ourselves that the purpose of the relationship as we have discussed it, namely, is the calling of one another into being.

Parents share with God the creative function. As we have seen, God is love. Having been created in His image, we need love and need to love, and we know one another best in the relationship of love. When we love, we are united and reunited with one another. In the special relationship of husband and wife our loving produces new life. This has religious meaning because our belief is that God created us out of love; and, as He did not create us to possess us, but left us free to be ourselves, so likewise parents produce their children, not to possess them, but to leave them free to become themselves. The work of parents, therefore, is to provide their children with the kind of relationship in which they may grow in the power of their own self-being, become their own person, and enter into their own responsible relation. This means that parents must be prepared to love their children and then relinquish them; and to rejoice in their growing up and in their increasing independence.

The task of the parents is not an easy one because it is not easy for us to love in a self-denying way. Actually, however, there turns out to be a surprising self-affirmation for parents who are willing to love their children and then let them go. And there is a good deal of self-loss for parents who try to love their children possessively and will not let them go. The latter parents are doomed to failure in the first place;

and secondly, the attempt to hold their children produces all kinds of unhappiness. On the contrary, when parents are able to let their children go as the final expression of their love for them, the chances are good that they will want to come back, and the relationship between parents and children will continue, though changed, and continue creatively. In time children may begin to understand the generosity of their parents' love, and parents may have the reward of seeing their children pass onto their children the same relatively selfless love. How can we become this kind of parent and what resources are there that will help us?

There are some factors that we can count on. The first is our power to recover from injury and to make adjustments even in the face of great odds. The human soul is not easily destroyed because our powers of survival are determined and persistent. This survival power of human nature should be a great comfort to us when we feel that we have done all the wrong things, and are afraid that we have injured the future of our children by our inept and blind efforts to help them. Of course, we should try to avoid as many serious mistakes as possible, but we know very well that we will make some, that we will hurt our children, and that if they were entirely dependent upon what we do for them, their future would indeed be dubious. However, all does not depend upon us alone. Not only are we active and responsible in the relationship, but our youngsters are active and responsible, too. They have within themselves creative possibilities of adjustment and of learning from their painful experiences. They may even gain added power from having to struggle and work through their experiences of deprivation, injustice, anxiety, hostility, and guilt.

Every teacher and parent needs to remind himself that his efforts to instruct and guide young people are complemented by their power of response. The power of pupils is just as great in its way as is the power of the teacher. Teachers and parents who count on this power will inevitably do a much better job, if for no other reason than that they will function with much less anxiety simply because they know they do not have to do it all.

The truth of this insight is always showing itself. It is rather obvious in the case of the child who is physically handicapped. With the right kind of encouragement, he can not only overcome his handicap, but do so in such a way that in some respects he may become stronger than he otherwise might. Then, there is the gifted person who seems to have come out of a most unpromising background, and we wonder how it could have happened. According to the theory of nurture, this seems like a miracle. Certainly a part of the explanation is to be found in the characteristic potential of human beings for creative response to hostile and limiting experiences. Particularly is this true if the experiences occur in the context of a relationship in which there is real evidence of being loved.

The mistakes that we make are not nearly as powerful as the love we give. That children can survive almost anything if they are truly loved has been illustrated so many times that it is a wonder we do not really believe it. If it were really believed, parents would not have to be as anxious as they are. They are anxious because they have more faith in the power of trying to do right than they have in the power of love. Yet we know that we cannot consistently do right and often do wrong. Many times we do not know what the right is that we would do. But if we genuinely love our children, their experience of our love will help them to overcome the effect of our mistakes.

Thus we see the creative power of love in the relationship of parent and child. Children need this kind of relationship when they reach their teens and are confronted by all the complex tasks of their development. Parents in their middle years need the reassurance of faith in the creative power of love in order that they may approach the complexities of their responsibilities with a sense of assurance.

Second, another factor that we can count on in carrying out parental responsibilities is that the love of our children is difficult to eradicate. Many parents are afraid they will lose the love of their children and often conclude because of the teenager's behavior, that they have already lost it. Their love has not been lost, it is only being reworked, in order that it may be re-expressed in ways that are appropriate to the changed circumstances and the maturity of adolescence. Most authorities are agreed that adolescents need their parents' love and confidence as much now as they ever did, even as much as in their earliest years, because of the disturbing changes that are occurring in them. Parents need to make sure, however, that they do not try to express their love in the ways that were appropriate earlier, nor should they expect the adolescent to express his love in the same old ways. His failure to do this is one reason why many parents fear that they have lost their youngster's love. Teenagers are self-conscious and do not like public display of affection between members of their family. In the expression of love it is wise to let them set the pace and style. Parents can afford to do this if they are assured that their children still love them. On the other hand, one needs to be prepared for variations in their expressions of love. At one time they may be very reticent and impatient of any display of affection. At another they may seem to want the love expressed as it was in childhood. This ambiguity can be very puzzling, and parents may not know what to expect or how to act.

All of this is but evidence of the radical transition through which they are passing. The last thing one should expect from adolescents is any kind of stability, dependability, or consistency. Actually their state of being is so fluid and uncertain that they do better with mature stable people who, because they are secure themselves, are able to accept this fluctuation and not be put off by the adolescent's inconsistencies. Moreover, adolescents should be taken seriously in the sense that what they are going through should be understood; but they should not be taken so seriously that they find themselves an obvious cause of worry. They want to be respected, but not fussed over.

Accordingly, parents can count on one thing: That their teenagers still need to be loved and need to love, and that they can survive all kinds of experiences which would seem to serve only to drive them away. Furthermore, we can be reassured that in spite of the things happening that would seem to separate and alienate us from one another, there is the indelible effect of the experience of past love and the ever present need of love. These are meanings that we can count on and which are resources for our relationship. But we should not take advantage of this fact and be careless about our relationship with them.

Third, parents should learn to expect, and to count on, the help that others can be to their children and realize that they are not alone in their responsibility.

During infancy and childhood parents provide their children with the primary relationship which is to serve for a number of years, for most of what infants and young children receive and learn is from their parents. From their parents children have their first experience of love and authority. As they grow older, other members of the family, teachers, playmates, classmates, buddies, and members of the opposite sex begin to provide experiences from which they learn a great host of things for both good and ill. Everyone influences them in one way or another. Thus, the responsibility for the child is increasingly spread among a number of people and resources. Parents can learn to think of these as providing things that they themselves could not hope to provide. This service of others may be regarded as complementary to the care of parents. In other words, the community as a whole is responsible for children, and fortunate are the parents who can carry out their responsibilities with a sense of the support and cooperation of the community in which they live.

This may seem like a hopeless ideal when one remembers the complex and fractured character of many communities. The condition of the community, however, does not excuse it from assuming its proper responsibilities. Therefore, churches and schools, city, county, and state organizations, health agencies, social service institutions, as well as parents and neighbors, should learn to think of their respective functions in relation to that done by others in behalf of children and young people. If parents and the other resources would, together, think about and work to fulfill their respective responsibilities, each could strengthen the other.

We have to face the fact that not all experiences with other people are helpful to children and adolescents. Indeed, many out-of-home experiences are quite destructive, and we must sometimes question how much parents can really count on the help of others. While we need to be as alert as possible to the kind of influence some outside experiences exert upon our adolescents, it does not follow that no value is to be drawn from these undesirable experiences. Adolescents are on the threshold of moving out of the family and assuming full responsibility for their own lives in a world in which the forces of good and evil are thoroughly

and often indistinguishably mixed. They need help in dealing with these mixed influences and in learning to respond
constructively and creatively to the various forces of evil
and their temptations. Now, one important function of a
teacher—and parents are teachers—is to help his students
learn from unfortunate and destructive experiences. For
instance, a boy may fall into the hands of a very self-
centered, ruthless, materialistic girl and be so seriously
disillusioned that his attitude toward women becomes dis-
torted and prejudiced.

On the face of it, this looks like a totally unfortunate
experience. And it could be, were it not that his parents
can help him think through the meaning of the experience
and see that he cannot take people for granted. He can
learn that all girls are not to be trusted, and that he needs
to be on guard against people who would exploit him.
Gradually, as a result of his experiences, this boy may become a more mature, responsible, and discriminating person
in understanding and dealing with various kinds of people.
Parents and others, then, can help young people change a
bad experience into a good one. For the most important
thing about these experiences is not what happens to the
individual, but what the individual is able to do about what
happens to him.

Fortunately, however, the influence of many people is
good, and parents should learn to count on this. There is
no more vivid illustration of this than the help that Jane
Foster had in her sickness from the artist, George Duncan.
He was able to do for her what her parents could not hope
to do, and made it possible for them to begin to help her.
This is always true in any ministry. The help that any two
people can be to someone cannot be measured by merely
adding together their efforts. For the ministry of one
strengthens the ministry of the other so that the total effect

is greater than this sum of their efforts. The family counselor to whom Bernard and his wife have gone is complementing, as well as giving direction to, Dick's and Julie's efforts to help their son. In other words, parents do not have to do everything by themselves. It is a comfort to us to realize that others can help us at the point where we feel most helpless. Thus, we should learn to think of others as complementary resources in the carrying out of our responsibilities. And, of course, we should remember that we can assist and complement their efforts, too.

iv

We turn now to steps that we can take toward meeting our responsibility to our older children. *First, through study, we can learn and understand more about adolescence.* There is usually great enthusiasm on the part of parents to study the care and feeding of infants and children. They read the writings of Benjamin Spock, Arnold Gesell and others, and they attend courses on children and their problems. When their children become adolescents, however, parents often fail to bring the same studious concern to the nature and problems of the teenager. As we have already remarked, there has not been as much material on this subject available for study, but there have always been available some good studies for those who wanted help. More and more books are now appearing on the nature and care of the adolescent. Popular magazines are constantly running articles on the subject, and various organizations and agencies are conducting courses designed to help parents meet their responsibilities.

The problem, however, seems to lie deeper than the level of materials and courses. We may not want to face the adolescent and his problems because they all too often activate our own. The experience of adolescence is often a painful one, the pain of which, for the most part, we mercifully forget. Our effort to understand and help our teenagers confronts us with the need to know and understand ourselves. Many of our unfaced and unresolved problems appear again. We may try to protect ourselves by evading any deeper knowledge or understanding of our adolescents. Our own lack of insight and maturity results in our becoming emotionally involved with them rather than in being able to help them. Another deterrent in helping adolescents is that we are afraid of them and their attitudes toward us. We do not like being called "old fogey's"—or even worse names. Parents have even been kept from joint action for fear of reprisals from their young.

The answer to our dilemma is to commit ourselves to a serious study of them and of ourselves. Our willingness to accept the pain of self-knowledge for the sake of insight will help us to achieve a sound relation with them. Knowledge and insight about them and ourselves, painful as it may be, cannot possibly be as destructive as our becoming emotionally and helplessly entangled with them. Parents may help themselves by getting together with other parents and with the help of descriptive and interpretive literature on adolescence undertake to learn to understand their charges and their responsibility to them. The process of sharing their concerns and discovering that they have common problems is a help. It is good for them to learn that their young people are the same as others, and that they are probably no better or worse than other parents. As a result of such reassurances, they are better able to make real progress together in their understanding of their young people and in their ability to help them.

Second, we can keep our relationship with them open at all costs. The worst thing that can happen to parents and children is for them to become so alienated from each other that they can no longer communicate. Earlier we saw the instance of the father who had to decide which was more important: the family car that had been wrecked or his son and their future relationship. Fenders and even whole cars can be replaced, but nothing can be done to restore relationship with one's son once the alienation has gone beyond a certain point. It would be more important to keep the relationship with the son.

Or, a girl may make very serious mistakes in the course of achieving her hetero-sexual maturity, but the mistake never justifies the rejection of her. This is also true from a religious point of view. Forgiveness is offered for every sin because the relationship between God and man is more important than any act of man against himself or his neighbor or God. To this end Christianity teaches that God is a forgiving God—the message of the Parable of the Prodigal Son and the Forgiving Father. The role of the parent is clear-cut at this point. Nothing is more important than the relationship between the parent and the child. No mistake, no act, nothing in fact, justifies the breaking off of the relationship. If we keep this in mind, it will help our perspective in times of crises. This does not minimize the disappointment and heart-ache that we may experience, but it will keep us from letting the disappointment and heart-ache blind us to the true issue, and, therefore, of our true responsibility and opportunity.

Third, we should be prepared to abdicate our responsibility and authority as fast as the child is able to assume responsibility for himself, and as rapidly as he is able to find within himself the authority by which he must live. We abdicate our rulership as the new ruler is able to take over. We have to be careful, however, that we do not abdicate before he is able to assume responsibility for himself. Some parents err in turning everything over to the adolescent who is not equal to running his own life. We cannot give a boy a man's job or ask a child to drive a car. Even though young people are gradually assuming responsibility for their own lives they still need a steadying hand, counsel, and the occasional restraint of authority.

This leads us to the fourth point which is that *we need to be prepared to exercise authority and to set the limits when needed.* Sometimes we parents are intimidated by the adolescent's violent rebellion against authority. The first thing to do is to make sure that the exercise of our authority is up to date or matches the capacities of our youngsters, and that we are not trying to administer the same kind of authority we did when they were five years younger. Then, we need to remember that it is only natural for adolescents' attitudes toward authority to be confused. And it is natural for them to mistake the amount of authority they are able to assume for themselves. Their attitudes toward authority sometimes grow out of the turmoil resulting from their declaration of independence and the achieving of autonomous, responsible selfhood. Often their reactions to authority are excessive because they feel unsure of themselves, and yet think they ought to feel sure of themselves. All this means that we have to determine the times and occasions when the teenager drives the car, how many nights he goes out, and help him manage his time for study and other responsibilities.

Furthermore, parents have to insist that responsibility accompany privilege. One of the outstanding characteristics of adolescents is that they are eager for every privilege, but singularly loathe to assume any responsibility. One creative way in which we can exercise our authority is by helping them to recognize and assume the responsibilities that go with the privileges they enjoy. If a son drives the car, he should also wash it and otherwise care for it. If he wants money to spend, he should earn at least some of it. If he does not earn, he cannot spend. Some may think this is ruthless treatment, but life is ruthless and the adolescent years are the time when the individual must begin to learn some of the sterner lessons of life if he is to be prepared for later experience. The time is rapidly passing when he can expect life simply to serve him. The time has come when he must begin to serve others.

This transition from the filial to the parental role is one of the major transitions that has to be accomplished in these years. Adolescents are making the change from being children who were cared for to adults who care for others. They move from being objects of love to being sources of love. This is a difficult transition for young people, and when they make it they need the help. It is not for their own good to be allowed to enjoy life without assuming responsibility for it.

Another way in which parents can aid their youngsters is by trying to help them arrive at the values by which they will live. In spite of their apparent rebellions and carelessness teenagers are asking questions that indicate that they are puzzled about values. What standards should guide their living? What is important in life? What does one really "go for"? Many parents have difficulty at this point because they do not know what their own values are. To conform and be accepted by the group seems at one time to be the important thing. Or the material advantages and resources of living seem to be the pearl of great price. Then there are other moments when they are drawn to the importance of the personal as against preoccupation with things. They feel the tension between the attractions of character and the need to please everyone. Parents who are confused about the important values in their life will not only confuse their young people but will be unable to help them work out their own problems in this area. This is the time when, if they have not done so before, they should seek to find a church and spiritual guides for themselves and for their children. Young people usually respect adults who are really seeking the truth and have a reverence for life. They do not expect adults to have all the answers and always to be right in every matter, but they do respond to mentors who are at least looking for God and His truths.

An aid to helping young people find the values by which they shall live is their ability to think and talk about important things. To be sure, they are not always in the mood to do so. But they have newly acquired powers of thinking and expression which they both need and want to use. And there is great healing to be had from talking about matters that either interest or trouble them. Our reason why more meaningful conversation does not take place between adults and teenagers is that the adult wants to do all the talking. They will not listen because it is hard for them to believe that youngsters have anything to say that is worth listening to. Because adolescents sometimes talk emotionally and irrationally, parents become so infuriated that the conversation breaks down. Sometimes it is necessary to let them rave and storm and say what they want and recognize that there is meaning behind it all. As soon as the youngsters discover that they are being heard they may begin to say what they really mean. Then parents may begin to have the heartwarming experience of real communication with their children on an adult level about matters of great meaning.

Finally, parents should remember that salvation comes from God and not from themselves. Too many parents are made anxious by their mistaken idea that they must be and do all things perfectly for their children. The most that we can be to them are helpers and guides. When we get right down to it, parents and children both are only fellow human beings. In adolescence, children discover how true this is of their parents. And parents are wise to acknowledge their common humanity and frailty with their teenagers and both turn and look to Him from whom all hope and love come. Out of these insights and with this help come the creative possibilities for relationship between parents and children.

CHAPTER 8

Your Work and You

"Wish I could get a better job. I'd like one where I could really influence the world. I'd like to accomplish something besides making a living—something worth while . . .

"Wish I had gone into politics as I'd planned. I knew about the corruption in politics, but I wasn't prepared for it. I couldn't accept it as a part of things nor did I know how to deal with it. I must have been pretty naïve. Anyhow, I couldn't play ball. Regretted it ever since. After all, the same conditions exist in every business. Wonder why youngsters can't be prepared for life in other than naïve or cynical ways. What good are ideals if they keep one from getting involved in the mess?

"It's tough when a guy's given his best and is squeezed out at the top. That's what I'm afraid of. And life is different for me now. New jobs don't come my way as often now, and life is narrowing down for me. It's sure hard to accept that the day of new adventures is almost over for me."

—Dick Foster

8   Our middle years are busy years, and the responsibilities and problems we face are many. The patterns of our family life are probably changing, with our children growing up, and their educational and social needs putting the family budget under a heavy strain. Although we may have arrived at the peak of our earning power or near it, our bills are probably higher and harder to meet than ever before. Our marriages may be giving us trouble. We may be carrying many church and community responsibilities. And on the job we are trying either to reach the top or to climb a little higher before we level off or drop back a step or two. We may feel the pressure of our more aggressive and imaginative younger associates who are working hard for advancement. We may even be a little intimidated by their youth.

But the middle years are productive years; and what we lack in power, speed, and glamour, we make up in experience, wisdom, and maturity. We are capable of a concentration and sustained effort that younger people rarely achieve. Moreover, we are also capable of intellectual application and continued mental growth as the large numbers of those from thirty-five to sixty successfully completing adult study courses evidence.

i

Work is an important area of life for those in their middle years. Yet Dick Foster and millions of others go to work day after day, earn some kind of living, and are frustrated by it. They commonly refer to their jobs as "the daily grind," speak of returning to the "salt mines," and in other ways indicate that their work is not a creative experience.

Is this frustration due so much to the nature of our work or to our failure to understand its meaning? We tend to conclude that the difficulty is due to the uncreative nature of the work. Indeed, we have set up in our minds a hierarchy of jobs in which some kinds of work are preferred to others. We think, for example, that mental work is more creative than manual work. That the executive has a better job than the staff worker. That the professions are more honorable than other kinds of work. These evaluations also force us to distinguish between persons on the basis of their function and thus lead to all kinds of false values. Is a man to be denied the privileges of creativity merely because he does not qualify as a professional person? or because he prefers to work with his hands? or because he is required to do so because of the circumstances of his life? Is the work of a mother and a housewife any less creative than that of her husband, directing from an office the affairs of a business or teaching the young in a classroom? When we reach a certain depth of understanding, it is utterly impossible for us to answer "yes" to these questions.

If a job is a necessary one and serves a purpose, it has meaning and justifies a man's doing it. Furthermore, only in doing such a job, can he have a sense of achievement Many people perform menial jobs, yet because they are aware, at least to some degree, of the purpose and meaning of their jobs, they are renewed in doing them. Others who have potentially creative tasks and yet are without this awareness may know nothing but frustration. Thus, we may conclude that the heart of this problem does not lie in the kind of work that we are doing but in our attitudes toward work.

These attitudes have been changing rapidly in the past few decades. Until quite recently men took pride in their work and strove to give dependable service or produce quality goods. Mr. Charles Brauer, an advertising man, was recently quoted in a LIFE editorial, as referring to our era as "the great era of the goof-off, the age of the half-done job. The land from coast to coast has been enjoying a stampede away from responsibility. It is populated with laundry-men who won't iron shirts, with waiters who won't serve, with carpenters who will come around someday maybe, with executives whose mind is on the golf course, with teachers who demand a single salary schedule so that achievement cannot be rewarded nor poor work punished, with students who take cinch courses because the hard ones make one think, with spiritual delinquents of all kinds who have been triumphantly determined to enjoy what was known unto the present crisis as the new leisure, and the salesman who won't sell, is only a part of this overall mess."

Small wonder a worker is bored with his job when there is meant to be a connection between his commitment to his task and the sense of achievement he may gain from it.

An examination of our motives for working is in order, for it is from this source that our problem may well stem. If we are working for the wrong reason, we shall never know a creative result. For instance, some of us work for the sake of working. Or, the job is used as an escape from other responsibilities: we find, for example, that the demands of our work are less threatening than our relationships with our families. Or, work may be for us the idol which we have set up to serve faithfully. But work is not a reason for living; rather should living be a reason for work. It is possible, of course, to enjoy working and to take pleasure in planning and executing one's work, but this alone is not a sufficient reason for working.

Then we may work for pay, for the money we can make from our efforts. Indeed, we may work only for remuneration and be easily drawn into exploiting ruthlessly from every situation and person the last cent that is to be had.

In such a case, the dollar sign becomes the expressive symbol of our relationships. The quality of our service or product will be only as good as is necessary to produce a monetary return. If we can get by without producing more than a minimum service, we will. Experience has shown, however, that a motive of profit does not open for us the creative experiences of work. True, remuneration is one of the motives for working, and we all need to earn a living adequate for our needs. But we must realize that the profit motive in itself cannot give meaning to our work.

Another motive for work that cannot produce creative results is that of working for the sake of status. Ambition has its place and even provides part of the incentive for doing creative work, but when work and the relationships in working are exploited for personal aggrandizement, the worker becomes guilty of manipulating others in the interest of his own success. This exploitation causes alienation and will ultimately preclude any truly creative results.

Then, too, our conception of work is perhaps unrealistic. As with Dick Foster, many of us are disillusioned because of the idealistic and naive expectations with which we approach the world and our part in it. We were unprepared, as was Dick, for the imperfection and corruption to be found everywhere; and like him, we want to wash our hands of the whole business. As corrupt as our political and economic systems are, however, they are not to be rejected because they are imperfect. They are still needed and useful; they still provide us, to an important degree, with protection against exploitation and make it possible for us to earn a living. Only by giving ourselves to the task that is ours, by accepting the injustice that is always a part of human life, and by assuming our responsibility to criticize and change the state of affairs in which men have to work, do we come eventually to the realization of the creative meaning of work. Many men have done creative work in situations that were imperfect and full of corruption.

What we need today, especially, is to grasp anew the biblical insight that we have to live and work under frustrating conditions, that our situation will never be an ideal one. Dick Foster needed help in realizing that tares grow with wheat, that injustice is always found with justice, and that we have to let the tares grow with the wheat until the harvest when they can be separated. So likewise, we often have to live with injustice and we become creative in the situation by facing that imperfection and corruption and trying to change that condition wherever possible.

Our attitudes toward the conditions of our work also keep us from realizing creative results. In the first place, there are today depersonalizing forces that change a man into a utility—an operator of a machine, a seller of goods, a keeper of accounts. These forces value chiefly the worker's function or utility and seem to disregard him as a person. This is hard for the worker to take because he is always a person. He naturally rebels and resents the attempt to downgrade him from a person to a thing. And while he is able, perhaps, to accept a quite subordinate role in the production effort, to permit his labor to serve a utility function, and to accept all this as a normal part of business and industrial life, yet he needs to be protected from its depersonalizing effects. If he is not secure, he may find that the only way he can endure being a pawn in this complex and impersonal world of business is by capitulating as a person and by hiding this indignity behind some mask—skill, position, reputation, wealth, or power. This response accounts only too well for the cynicism that exists so widely among the workers of the world, whether they be professional, executive, or manual. Deep down, they are suffering from the loss of personal meaning in their work.

Another condition of modern employment that affects work attitudes is the conformity which a mechanistic system demands. Millions of workers, whether mechanical or managerial, are caught up in a great machine in which the worker has only his fragmentary part to play and in which he must perform without any margin for personal variation so as not to disturb the functions of others or the operation of the machine. Continued life in this kind of system will destroy creative potential, for creativity is always seeking new forms of expression. The injunction "You are not being paid to think but to do as you are told" applies in our day not only to men on the assembly line but to all kinds of workers. And although many industries are constantly seeking suggestions from their workers and striving to excite and benefit from their creativity, most of us tend to get caught up in this enslavement to machines and systems.

The following quotation may be understood both figuratively and literally: "While the engine runs, people must work. Men, women, and children are yoked together with iron, steam, electricity, and atomic energy. Men who are breakable and subject to a thousand sources of suffering are chained to machines of steel which know no suffering or weariness." It is easy for us to feel today that we are caught in the maw of process and that we are being relentlessly destroyed by mechanization.

And yet systems and machines may be used creatively and provide a certain stability and security. They can help to supply opportunity for the free play of creative expression in that we do not have to spend time and energy working out the mechanics for basic living. Therefore, our task is really to achieve a balance between the stability and security of this system and the destructive effect of its ruthless operation.

Closely related to the situation we are examining and in

part, perhaps, stemming from it is the one where we find ourselves stifled and confused by the complexity, mobility, pace, and uncertainty of business and professional life. That this is a source of wide anxiety and the cause of many breakdowns is clearly evident to anyone who has read the records of patients in our general and mental hospitals.

Still another condition with which we must cope is that of the moral ambiguity and confusion of our time, and the feelings of guilt which these awaken in us. This condition is generally acknowledged in the frequently heard statement that one cannot, at the same time, be a good Christian and a good business man. The statement, of course, reveals an unreal conception of both the Christian and the business man. For in that statement the Christian is conceived as someone who always does the right things; and the business man as one who, because he cannot always do the right thing, cannot be a Christian. But a business man who is a good Christian knows that there may be conflicts between what his job requires of him and what his Christian faith requires. He knows that, in all occupations, there are occasions when the reconciliation of Christian faith and practice, with the dictates or procedures of the world, may be hopelessly difficult to accomplish. He expects to find himself caught between the pull of two commitments—his commitment to God's will and his commitment to his business. Indeed, his Christian role may well be to accept and live with the conflict, to strive for the reconciliation of his commitments, knowing that ultimately he is dependent upon God's forgiveness rather than upon his own perfect obedience.

But what does "accepting and living with the conflict, and striving for the reconciliation of commitments" mean? It means that in those situations out of which he cannot walk and in which he must act, even though he is definitely limited by the outward situation with respect to his choice of action and even though his action cannot be defended in every respect as the action of a Christian—it means that in such situations, the Christian business man can still act in a profoundly Christian way. At those moments he will not deceive himself by thinking what is good for his business is good for God. He will face squarely the fact that his action is not a good deed. But because he wants to do that which is good, he acknowledges God's sovereign rule, his own feeble and limited power of action—"that of ourselves we can do no good"—and with contrite heart he does what he must, trusting God in His mercy to save him and all men. This man is reconciled to God because he deplores that which circumstance demands of him and because with faith he looks forward for salvation to God's judgment and the coming of His Kingdom. This man, let it be noted, is not reconciled to the action he finds himself forced to take. Indeed, some other time, later, he may find the opportunity to do something about such situations, to eliminate them from the business world. But at the moment he can do only what is open to him—do it and trust in God. In wartime the soldier finds himself in a similar position—he has his commitment to obey the commandment as well as his commitment to defend family, home, and nation.

People often represent the Christian position as being one in which we maintain a Christian stand and take the consequences, even to being fired or losing our business. This is not the only alternative. There may be times when this kind of witness is necessary, but the Christian may be called to remain in the battle, to do the best he can, and to accept and endure the conflict which may never be eliminated. This is often the more heroic role, the one in which the witness for God is more impressive.

In other words, the moral ambiguity of our modern business and professional life is something that is to be lived with and accepted as a challenge to our Christian witness. Instead of running away from life, we are called upon to dig in and witness where the issue is being fought.

Finally, as our civilization becomes more complex and the processes of production become more mechanized and automated, the separation between the worker's effort and the product is increased. This reduces for him the possibility of direct satisfaction from his creative effort. Not many of us are engaged in the whole process of production as is the farmer or as was the craftsman of a former day. Sometimes there is no visible evidence of the effort we have put into turning out a product. Even people who are engaged in the more creative occupations, particularly those who work with people, often lack a sense of accomplishment. The results of their labors are not clear-cut and may never be seen even though they exist. Mothers complain of the repetitive daily grind that seems to be rewarded only by the rebellion of her charges. This absence of a sense of accomplishment (which is all too prevalent) stifles the creative spirit, and we tend to become discouraged and uninspired. Gradually we are seduced into taking the line of least resistance and capitulate to boredom.

These conditions are inevitable and will be found to accompany almost any kind of work. No amount of change can ever completely eliminate them. So, once again, we are faced with the necessity of accepting the nature of life, and the way in which much of its work has to be done. This acceptance is much more healthy than the naive expectation that such conditions should not exist. But it is also important that we try to change the conditions that prevent and destroy creative results from our work. And we can change our attitude towards these conditions. We can abandon our former unrealistic and naive expectations and assume a more mature attitude toward life and the conditions in which its work must be done. How are we to go about this?

Sometimes we can find sources of substitute satisfaction. Various hobbies are a help in this respect. Gardening, for instance, restores to modern man the age-old satisfactions of planting, tending, and reaping. Hobbies that give men and women opportunity to work skillfully with their hands yield the satisfactions that craftsmen used to enjoy. These resources, and others like them, are creative means which will help us to endure the ambiguity, uncertainty, and even absence of satisfaction in our routine labors.

ii

We come now to the question of how can we change our attitudes toward our daily work and toward the world in which we have to work. *The first change must come in our attitude toward ourselves as persons in a world of things.* When we go to work, we enter a world of things. We have seen previously in this chapter that one of our problems in relation to work is that we as persons resent being used as, and reduced to the status of, things. Rather than resent this person-thing dilemma, we should expect it. Every person has functions, functions which are necessary to other people. Other people have a right to expect us to function in ways beneficial to them, even as we have a right to expect that they be willing to function in ways that contribute to the richness of our life. There exists a great deal of confusion on this point. The current emphasis on the importance of the personal encounter between man and man has been seriously misinterpreted to mean that anything that is not personal is wrong and sinful. We need to remember that an intimately personal relation cannot be maintained constantly. Much of our time is devoted to the business of living in which our relation to one another is relatively impersonal and functional. The sin is not in living functionally but in living that way without any expectation of meaningful personal encounter. We should so carry on our business, and relate to each other as we carry on our functions, that the possibility of finding each other as persons always exists. When such is the case, the occasions of personal encounter will greatly increase.

Furthermore, we have reason to consent to entering this world of things when we go to work, in that we do so with the expectation both that we shall be used and that we shall use others. And we have no reason for being unwilling to perform our function since we are continually dependent upon and use the functions of others. This type of reciprocity is present in every kind of work. In other words, we live for one another and gladly work for one another with the expectation that personal concerns will not, for the moment, be central. Therefore, the more mature a person is, the better he is able to make the commitments that are necessary to the world's work.

On the other hand, immature people often interfere with important work because their energies are spent in finding security for themselves rather than in doing their job. Whenever possible, the wise employer avoids hiring them, for they are so threatened by the function demanded of them that they cannot be efficiently useful. But a mature, secure person can accept that demand without the feeling that his person is thereby limited or threatened.

This person, while accepting the demand to function, is, however, rightly on his guard against any effort to exploit him or any failure to respect his integrity as a person. He is intolerant of corruption and injustice, and will try to protect himself and others from them. Or, to use the language of an earlier chapter, the power of the personal is able to operate in and through the impersonal organizations of life. It is able to deal with "things" and survive as the personal. Because of our power as persons, we may engage in our work in such ways that we look for, and respond to, the persons with whom we work. The insidious danger is that we frequently organize our work in such a way that we become blind to the personal which is always potentially present. For example, Phil Johnson, a member of the seminar on "The Christian and His Job," maintained that, in the broker's office where he worked, there was no place for the personal, and that, so far as he could see, he had no personal responsibility for the people associated with him. The purpose of a business office, he maintained, was to conduct its affairs efficiently, and to that end people were a means. After several weeks, he became aware of a young woman in the office who had been causing a good deal of difficulty. Finally, it occurred to him that she might be causing the difficulty because of some kind of personal trouble. The responsibility became his to talk with her about the effect she was having on the office organization. As a result of his seminar discussions and experience he found himself talking to her as a person rather than a worker. And he discovered that her effect upon the other workers was owing to her problems in private life. Since she was able to confide in him, she was greatly helped and began to function more adequately.

Though as persons we enter into the world of things and willingly participate in an exchange of functions, yet at any moment we may be called upon to hear and respond to other persons in personal, rather than functional, ways. At any moment, on the job, we may break through the impersonal and find ourselves standing face to face in some meaningful, personal encounter. A Christian accepts the discipline of being a responsible person in the world of things-and-functions, and yet he expects to be summoned by, and respond to, the personal. He expects to break through the *it* to the *Thou* for whom he engages in responsible work. Thus it is that God may find us in our daily work, and we may find God.

A second corrective to our attitude toward work is to accept it because it is socially necessary and meets some aspect of human need. The purpose of our work is not entirely that it should give us an emotional lift and be personally satisfying, but rather that it be a necessary part of the world's work. If work contributes to the common good, then it is necessary, and the service of the workman who does the work is necessary. In rendering his service faithfully he is living creatively and participating with the creativity of others.

All necessary work is worthy of the worker, and the distinctions we make between such jobs must be regarded, on serious thought, as somewhat superficial. Not all people want prominent work, nor do they want, or are they capable of, public or heavy responsibility. Many prefer obscurity and want to do their share of the world's work quietly and inconspicuously. But all workers, regardless of their jobs, should be helped to understand the significance of what they are doing. Certainly the world needs the faithful influence, whether known or hidden, of every worker's devotion to his task.

When we have said this, however, we must still face the fact that there are some jobs that serve no useful purpose and cannot, by any stretch of charity, be fitted into a Christian way of life. To this problem Stephen Bayne, in his book *Christian Living*, gives the one possible answer—*get out of it as quickly as you can.*

A third corrective to our attitude toward work is to see

it as a part of God's work. All work that contributes to the common good is God's. According to the Bible, God is known by His action in the actual every day business of living, of social relationships, and of current historical events. The worker, therefore, serves God by doing faithfully His work. By our work we participate in God's creation in many ways. The study and experimentation that opened up our knowledge of nuclear physics is an example of the creative powers God has given us. We might be tempted to think that the creativity shown in that discovery belonged only to the scientists who directly engaged in the study and experimentation. But all mankind, directly and indirectly, shared in the discovery. The executives and the workers of the various manufacturing companies that produced the materials with which the scientists worked; the federal, state, and local officials who kept the machinery of government going; the personnel of hospitals and social agencies; the milkman, the tailor, the minister, the plumber, the garbage collector, the street sweeper—all worked together to create a community with resources and stability that made possible such a study and such a discovery. All participated significantly in this creative act, and each man's work was necessary to every other man's work. The faithfulness of one man was just as important as that of others. For each by his faithfulness to his particular task was imitating Christ who was faithful in His task of saving the world. There are differences in tasks, but faithfulness is faithfulness, no matter what the task.

This concept provides us with a context and perspective for all work. It stands as a corrective to the tragic misconceptions about work that riddle our culture. Indeed, the misconception most common among people with a religious commitment is that only church work is God's work and that only by doing church work may one hope to serve

God. One evidence of this viewpoint is that many men think that the only way they can be sure of serving God is by studying for the ordained ministry. But that is a viewpoint that contradicts the conception of work that we have been discussing, namely, that all work is God's work and that by the faithful performance of it we serve God.

Many mothers and housewives are victims of a similar misconception. They are notoriously unhappy and frustrated because they do not see, and are often not helped to see, the significance of their work. This does not mean that they should confine their interests and activities to housework, but it does mean that their work should produce more satisfaction and sense of meaning than it commonly does. Many of them engage in club or church work in order to escape the boredom of their daily grind. They—indeed many of us—have allowed boredom with the daily routine to blind them to the meaning of what is accomplished through that routine.

When we see our particular job in its relation to the whole creation and to the whole creative process of living, it ceases to be a job and begins to be a means through which we may express ourselves. Two boys, both of them from a community in which was located a large airplane factory, were interviewed for attendance at a summer camp. One boy was asked by the counselor, "What does your father do?"

"Oh, he's just a riveter," he replied.

The other boy, when asked the same question about his father who also was a riveter, replied, "He builds airplanes!"

The reply of the second boy points up for us the difference between a job and a vocation. Although his father participated in only a single step in the total production process, the riveting, he was, nonetheless, a builder of airplanes. Work may be routine and uninspiring, but it always has meaning, and it is there for anyone with eyes to see it.

This same truth was impressed upon me one beautiful day as I stood waiting for a streetcar, on the corner of a big, busy, dirty city. I noticed two street cleaners, one on each side of the street, moving slowly toward me as they brushed the dirt into piles along the gutters. One was doing his job well, the other wasn't. When the man on my side of the street came abreast of me, I commented on the neat job he was doing. He glanced at me in surprise. Then, looking back over his work, he said in his broken English, "She do looka good, huh?" Then, he pointed to the blue sky overhead and said, "God's world, she very beautiful. Me, I gotta go to work." With that he went on down the street sweeping into neat piles the refuse of a careless city.

There went a man with a menial job but a powerful sense of vocation, and the menial job had somehow become the means by which he pursued his vocation. For, somehow, he knew that a street cleaner serves God by being a good street cleaner. Moreover, by his witness he unknowingly taught that lesson to hundreds of people by teaching it to me. For I, as a professional teacher, have passed it on to others to make part of their wisdom. A job, any job that serves a constructive purpose, even a menial job, has the meaning of a ministry; and by our faithfulness to it, we serve both God and man.

We can now begin to see how important the worker is to the work. The quality of the work and its significance as a free contribution to life is not dependent upon the nature of the work but upon the character of the workman. This is clearly true in the story of the two street cleaners and in the two boys' different appraisals of their fathers' jobs.

Yet we allow the impersonal character of much of the world's work to obliterate or overshadow the significance of the person of the worker. Certainly when we stand on the overhead walk, looking down upon the massive machinery, row upon row, that stamps sheets of metal into automobile fenders, it seems as if the man who operates those machines is engulfed by them. Yet, we need to remember that without the man, the machine is helpless. It is only with the man's direction that the machine becomes an efficient instrument of unbelievable productiveness and creativity. The person makes the thing and, therefore, has power over it; he becomes slave to the thing only because he allows the thing to become master over him. When the person and the thing *combine creatively,* they accomplish what neither alone can. There is danger in the mechanization of life, but also potential for tremendous creativity.

⋯
iii

It may surprise us to discover that the Christian ministry, which has so many creative possibilities for service, is often an illustration of how work can become a thing that enslaves the worker. This occurs because the work of the ministry is dependent upon the institutional existence and organization of the church. The needs of this organization can become so demanding that its leaders and members are preoccupied with the organization's existence and forget the reasons for its existence. Little by little, laymen and clergy alike become the slaves of the institution. Thus the fellowship becomes a thing that enslaves its members. The redemptive purpose of the ministry is swallowed up by our servitude to the parochial idol.

No work is safe from the danger of being gobbled up by impersonal organization, mechanization, systematization.

Another corrective of man's work and the conditions under which it is done comes through our willingness to challenge and change the work and its conditions. No one has the right to criticize and judge our social order who does not work faithfully and hard. A person who will not assume his political responsibilities has no right to criticize politics. People who will not have anything to do with the church have no right to criticize the church for what it fails to do. Only the faithful and committed person is justified in raising his critical voice. Every honest worker has the responsibility also to be concerned about the social, political, and economic conditions in which men exercise whatever freedom they have to choose their work and to pursue it. Obviously, in a culture as complex as ours, it is necessary for the individual to join himself with those groups in which his voice can be magnified by its union with others. Developments in our own country show how effective this can be. Labor unions grew up as organizations within which men joined together to secure protection and justice for the worker. In so doing, they stood in judgment on all those organizations that had responsibility for the inhuman conditions under which men worked. Thus the workers who were members of the union had the responsibility under God not only to do their work, but to change the character and condition of that work as well. Now the unions need to accept the same judgment wherewith they judged others. For they, too, can cease to be a means to an end and become ends in themselves and enslavers of men's loyalties. Every movement that is called into being to judge and correct the institutions and orders by which men live must, in its turn, be judged lest its purposes be corrupted. It does not follow, however, that because these purposes are subject to corruption, men should cease to band together to assume critical responsibility for the conditions of human life.

Men and women who are in their middle and creative years have had the experience and possess the maturity that qualifies them to raise thoughtful questions about the purpose of their own and others work and to seek answers to their questions. By working together through natural groups such as labor unions, political organizations, professional groups, community associations, Parent-Teachers Associations, and the like, Christian people may influence the efforts of men as they seek to improve the economic, social, and political orders.

It is unfortunate that more churches are not helping people to think through the meaning of their work. A strange separation seems to exist between what goes on in the church on Sunday and what people do on the other days of the week. Sermons are preached, urging people to follow Christ and to witness to His truths, but this exhortation is often made in the abstract without definite suggestions and without provision for any kind of study group to help people translate the exhortation into concrete terms. Many laymen confess that they leave this kind of an experience in church, and returning to their work, become so engrossed in their business activity that they never think of church again until it is time to reappear there.

At this point we once again run into the old conception that religious work is church work and that our daily work is secular. We have already seen thus far that we cannot hope to do that work which is to serve God and man except as we do it in the areas of our most significant living, one of which is in our daily work. When we fail to help people consider the meaning of their work in the light of religious teaching, we are failing both God and man. The Church's true task is not to minister to itself but to minister to men in the condition in which they live and work.

A recovery of this true mission of the Church is being nurtured by the evangelical academies of Europe, The World Council of Churches, and by such pioneer movements as The Detroit Industrial Mission and Parishfield. Their

concern is expressed in the following statement of the
World Council of Churches at Evanston, 1954: "The real
battles of the faith today are being fought in factories,
shops, offices, and farms, in political parties and government agencies, in countless homes, in the press, radio and
television. . . . Very often it is said that the church should
go into these spheres; but the fact is that the church is
already in these spheres in the persons of the laity."

Not long ago I heard a minister complain that his church
was growing so fast there was not enough work around the
church to give everyone something to do so that he might
engage in Christian service. Apparently it had never occurred to him to think of the work his people do in the
world as a way in which they might render service to the
world in the name of God; or to set up a training program
in which they would be helped to see and use their opportunities.

A local church can also set up vocational study programs
to give its people the opportunity to study and discuss together how they might do their daily work as Christians.
Housewives and mothers are greatly helped by meeting
together to consider their common problems and the possibilities that are open to them for creative accomplishment
in their daily work. Factory workers have been happy to sit
down together under the leadership of a spiritual guide who
is able to help them think through the meaning of their
daily work in relation to the teachings of their faith. Indeed,
the same will be true of any group, whether it be of doctors,
teachers, or business people, since most of these people are
in their creative years and looking for ways in which to
exercise their creativity. We have already seen how the
worker with a vision can transform a job. If, then, it is the
responsibility of religion to transform the person, it ought to
do so in terms of his daily responsibilities.

One of the exciting experiences of my ministry was meeting with a group of people who for the most part had an uninspired attitude toward their daily work. They were devoted members of the church who felt that church work was the only way in which one served God. As they met together over the months, their whole conception of this relation changed so that they began to see their daily life as an opportunity for the expression of their Christian faith. They became more aware of the people with whom they were working as persons and of their personal responsibility for them. They began to see the situations in which they found themselves in their daily life and work, as occasions when, in quiet and meaningful ways, they could witness to truth and right. They readily acknowledged that previously they had been careless and indifferent about their witness in this respect. Now they became more concerned about the policies that lay behind the work they were given to do, and their work thereby became more interesting to them.

A corollary of this was that their worship on Sunday also became more meaningful. Out of their work they brought needs and experiences that made it possible for them to enter more meaningfully the fellowship of people who were offering to God themselves and their lives, and in return were receiving forgiveness and renewal in order to return to their respective duties. This corollary is important because as long as there is a separation between worship and life, the worship remains unreal and formal. It has been demonstrated again and again that people who have a sense of vocation about their work are people who bring great meaning to their worship and, in turn, are strengthened by it.

Another way in which the church can help people find renewed creativity in their daily life and work is by helping them to see the opportunities they have for Christian service in their existing relationships. Too often we urge people in the name of Christian service to undertake something new which may not be as important as the thing they are already doing. I am reminded of the woman who, persuaded by her minister, gave up her work in the League of Women Voters in order to teach a Sunday School class. To be sure the class needed a teacher, but this woman was engaged in an activity that gave her opportunity to minister as a Christian and a church member to the political and social life of her community. Someone else who did not have her special opportunity surely could have been found to teach the faith to the young which, of course, is equally important.

The same thing is true of people who serve on the boards of institutions and agencies that are rendering public service. This should be regarded just as much a part of the work of the church as serving on an altar guild, in a women's organization, or in the session or vestry. Furthermore, these people need and for the most part welcome help in meeting these responsibilities out of the insights and other resources of their Christian faith.

A woman who did volunteer work in a hospital and who regarded it as her "church work" reported that not only was she able to help the patients but that staff members and other volunteer workers became interested in, and responded to, the Christian motive and purpose of her service. The public preaching and teaching of the church needs to guide its members in this direction more than it does; and its study programs should be helpfully focused on the areas in which these people serve.

The purpose of all work, therefore, is to serve God and man. All work is to be judged according as it serves this purpose. If the work does, then the worker may freely give himself to it, knowing that in serving the work he is serving God. Here is a concept of work for the middle years when men and women are doing their most creative work.

9

From Security to Maturity

"It seems that we're all concerned about security, but it looks to me as if our concern for it is turning us into cowards. I'm afraid to be myself because I'd be different, and everybody's agreed that if you're different from others, you'd be lonely. Somebody said that if you wanted to belong, you'd have to give up your integrity.

"Why should we have to conform to be a member of a group? We shouldn't have to junk ourselves in order to belong. Like my office, the group becomes a monster that feeds on a man. That's what our staff organization is becoming—a monster that's saying, 'If you want to be a part of me, you'll have to be a mouse, and don't criticize me.' I'd sure like to call the brute's bluff! I sometimes think the best thing I could do would be to stand up for what I believe, take the consequences, even if it meant the ax. Maybe I'd get my self-respect back. Maybe Julie'd respect me again. Who knows, I might get a better job! It'd take guts to do this. After all, I'm 45, and the younger crowd is pushing me hard! God, it's hard to choose between playing it safe and growing up."

—Dick Foster

9 All of us face in life the necessity of growing out of the security preoccupations of childhood to the maturity occupations of adulthood. Not that security ceases to be important to us as mature people; far from it, for security is always a necessary condition for living. But it means that we must not make an occupation or career out of achieving security; we do that only of living and growing.

When we were children, it was exciting to measure ourselves against yardsticks and door jambs to see how much we had grown. But we stopped doing that when we grew up, for at that point a let-down occurred. It was almost as if the excitement of growth were no longer possible to us, as if there were nothing left to live for any more. This chapter is about a kind of growing that is more exciting than that which has to do with added inches of stature; it is about rewards which, while not as easy to come by as a new dress or suit, are more satisfying and lasting.

Many of us miss this new kind of growing because of insecurity and anxiety. As Dick Foster noted, many people in our time are preoccupied with security as a goal. Only that morning he had interviewed a young man who was applying for a job in his company. After he had explained to him the kind of work he would do and had described the kind of opportunity he would find, Dick asked the young man if he had any questions. Immediately, the applicant replied, "Tell me about your pension plan." This young man was so concerned about security at the beginning of his life that he was more interested in the conditions of his eventual retirement than in his present opportunities.

i

Everywhere we find evidences of this preoccupation with security. Some of our characteristic phrases are indicative of it: "organization man," "corporation wife," "group concerns," "party line." "Don't stick your neck out if you don't have to." "Don't say anything that can be held against you!" There is widespread today throughout our society a desire to be accepted by the group at any price, an unwillingness to show individual traits, and a willingness to accept limited happiness rather than to face serious risks.

Even preaching in the churches sometimes appeals to us in terms of fears and insecurities. This is a strange corruption of a faith that advertises its transforming power: "Do not be conformed to this world, but be transformed by the renewal of your mind" (*Romans* 12:2, RSV). Instead of being called to challenge the *status quo* and evil, men are lulled by some religious teachers into a condition of adjustment—if not one of utter passivity. The kingdom of security has become the fellowship of the new "saints" of our generation! Indeed, one of the chief ways in which we seek to gain security is by conforming to the expectation of others.

Conformity becomes, in our minds, the source of security. One reason given for the increase of juvenile delinquency is that parents are so eager for their children to be popular and successful that they do not exercise the controls and administer the disciplines which might develop character power in their children. When adolescents ask for permission to do something that arouses the anxiety of parents, the latter often give consent if other parents are doing so. We look to others for signals as to what we should think or do. Gradually we lose the freedom and courage to act independently when the need arises. We live in a time when we give eager lip service to individuality and integrity, but we really serve conformity and popularity.

Technical civilization tends to make men into objects caught up in a machine of production and consumption. Even our children become cogs in the machine and are referred to as "consumer trainees." Our "culture" is organized to convince our children that they must satisfy their needs, or they will not belong or be secure. We are now so organized that manipulation of man by man is inevitable. Aldous Huxley's *Brave New World,* George Orwell's *1984,* and similar novels portray the results of our present tendencies toward conformity, in showing the average man as being without a will of his own and under the domination and direction of a machine-like government. It is interesting to note, however, that under this kind of regimen designed to meet the needs of people and provide them with unbroken security, there arises in them a deep sense of anxiety and insecurity.

"The tide of organization in our private life may engulf the last surviving instinct to preserve the safeguards of individual freedom," writes President A. Whitney Griswold of Yale. He goes on to attack "the endless, sterile, stultifying conferences held in substitution . . . for individual inventiveness; the public opinion polls whose vogue threatens even our moral and aesthetic values with the pernicious doctrine that the customer is always right; the unctuous public relation counsels that rob us both of our courage and our convictions. This continuous daily deferral of opinion and judgment to someone else becomes a habit . . . . It conjures a nightmare picture of a whole nation of yes-men, of hitch-hikers, eavesdroppers, and peeping toms, tiptoeing backward off-stage with their fingers to their lips . . . . symptoms of a loss of self-respect by people who cannot respect what they do not know. They do not know themselves because they spend so much of their time listening to somebody else." [1]

A recent editorial in a popular magazine characterized many of our generation as yes-men eager to accept faceless and voiceless roles in a world that submits without protest to conformity. And, it is true! The price for the kind of security for which many are now looking is conformity! We fear to ask questions that disturb the *status quo*. But failure to ask questions destroys creativity. As someone has said: "We can make machines that *answer* questions, but we cannot make machines that *ask* questions." Unless questions are asked, answers will not be found, as we shall see later.

Does this discussion suggest that there is no place for security concerns? Obviously the answer is "No." Security is a necessary condition for growth and living. Children must feel, and be, secure. It is necessary for their growth and development as persons, for their acquisition of skills, and for confidence in their employment of them. As a result of their experience of security, they may become persons with courage to live and to give themselves in all the relationships of life. And we continue to need, during our adult years, security in all the crucial areas of life. But, beyond a certain point, we can value security so highly as to become afraid to do anything that involves risk. When that happens, security—a condition necessary for living—has become the end and goal of life.

Security is not the goal of life. It is not a destination. Nor should it be the prize for which we work. Even Dick, in his unhappy confusion, could see that security was a dull sort

---

[1] A. Whitney Griswold, *In the University Tradition* (New Haven: Yale University Press, 1957), p. 159: The Yale Baccalaureate, June 9, 1957. Quoted with permission.

of goal. If we make the achievement of security our chief aim, we lose the meaning of life. "Whoever will save his life will lose it." (*Matthew* 16:25, RSV)

Security is a starting point, not a destination. It is the platform from which to launch into creative living and work. Its principle is: "Whoever loses his life . . . will find it." With true inner security, one faces the risks of life. But true inner security is renewed by giving oneself to these very risks. For instance, the man of faith, out of the strength he has from his faith, is able to face the great and perplexing questions of life and accept the inevitable moments of anxiety and insecurity. The courageous pioneer must have had, sometime in his life, some experience of security else he would not now be able to pioneer.

We can see from this that security is not something to be saved, but rather something to be spent. We do not accumulate security for the sake of being secure, but in order to give ourselves, out of our experience of security, to the occupations, relationships, and challenges of life.

If all has gone well during nurture and development, we move more easily through the doorway of security into the life of maturity. Most of us, however, have not moved easily through the doorway. But from this it does not follow that the door is closed to us. We can still learn to give ourselves and, to that extent, achieve a maturity that *is* a source of inner security.

The contradictions of adolescence are a good illustration of the conflict within the individual between the desire to be cared for and the desire to grow up and to take care of others. It is good to have someone take care of us and to protect us from the dangers, complexities, and demands of life. Furthermore, there are outside forces that keep us immature. Parents, especially mothers, have mixed feelings about their babies growing up. They want to keep them babies, but they also want them to become men and women who marry and take their place in life. Because of these conflicting impulses and forces the process of becoming mature, even at best, is accompanied by a struggle.

Here we need to remind ourselves of our theme: that we should move from the security preoccupations of the child to the maturity occupations of the adult. I say we "should" because this is the law of life. It is written into our very nature. And it is a law that can be illustrated clearly. For instance, babies begin life entirely dependent, irresponsible, and egocentric. (These words are used descriptively and without any suggestion of moral failure.) But, in the course of a very few years, they become more independent, responsible, and altruistic. Likewise, they begin life in a completely filial relationship, and in a very few years they must be able to assume a parental one. In the beginning of their lives, they are largely victims of circumstance and environment. But, as they grow older and mature, they are able to change circumstance and influence environment. They also begin life unconscious of themselves as persons, of others, or of the world into which they are born. As they grow older, they become increasingly conscious of themselves and others. In the beginning of their lives, it is intolerable for them to be ignored, but as they grow older and become more mature, they are more able to accept an absence of attention and even learn to sacrifice themselves for others or for a cause.

Caution is needed at this point, however. The achievement of maturity is always relative. That is, no matter how mature we may become, we are still immature. No one can say, "I am mature." The most we can hope is that we shall continue to mature, but we must always be prepared for times when we backslide, for times when we feel insecure and vulnerable. When we are sick, for instance. we are likely

to become immature, helpless, and demanding. When someone hurts us, we may find ourselves responding more
childishly than usual. We should not be surprised at these
occasions, nor hold ourselves under too severe judgment
because of them. They should be accepted as signs of our
humanity. If we recover and resume a more responsible way
of living, these times of regression will not be serious. The
memory of them will help keep us humble, from being too
proud of our assumed maturity.

ii

Maturity is the measure of the quality
of our relationships and of the way in which we live them.
These relationships are so complex, however, that it is difficult for us to know what their condition is. Particularly
do we need some kind of standard by which to evaluate
the part we are playing in this maze of relationships and responsibilities. Conscientious people used to be guided in
their living by literature that might be variously named:
"Guides to Spiritual Living," "How to Be Religious,"
"Principles for the Practice of Devout Life," "How to Be a
Christian," and others. These criteria are still used by
thousands of people and are invaluable aids to them. But,
there are also many thousands of people for whom such
guides are meaningless. The traditional religious words and
exercises do not continue to have meaning for them, and
yet they are conscientious people who seek to dedicate
themselves seriously to their responsibilities. They may not
be religious in an overt, formal way, but their spirit is a
devout one. We all need criteria to guide us in living. Even
those who use the more traditional guides can be helped
by reference to another kind of criteria having a different
approach to the meaning of their religious life. We turn
now to consider some of these guides for responsible living.

First, however, a word of warning: The following guides of maturity may seem like counsels of perfection, but they should not be viewed as such. Instead, we may regard them as beacons, navigational aids, as it were, to help us move through the tricky waters of life. They are not laws to be obeyed, but guides for growing.

First, we are mature to the extent that we are guided by our long-term purposes rather than by our immediate desires.

When we were children, feelings played a big part in our lives and often determined our actions. We were emotional, and our behavior often irrational. As we grew older, however, we began to acquire some ability to discipline our feelings and to control our actions according to more or less considered purposes. Adolescence is a difficult time for both the adolescent and the adult because it is the age at which childish and adult ways of living collide in the adolescent— feelings and larger purposes conflict.

Even when we become relatively mature, there is always the danger that our feelings, like pirates, will capture and dominate us, cause us to make decisions and do things we shall later regret. For instance, feelings of depression may cause us, if we are not on guard, to abandon a project just when it might turn out successful. On the other hand, toward given goals men have worked for years in spite of all kinds of discouragements from within and without, because they were governed not by their feelings but by their sense of purpose. Feelings of discouragement and alienation may cause us to break a marriage partnership, when a more mature approach to marriage would be to recognize that the achievement of a marriage is a lifelong purpose in the pursuit of which our feelings at various times will be both for and against it. Again, anyone who has undertaken creative work knows that there are moments when his feelings counsel him to abandon his efforts, but that he continues because of the sense of purpose which gives him the power to rise above those less dependable feelings and attitudes.

An essential element in pursuing long-term purposes is a willingness to give up momentary pleasures for the sake of more lasting values. The child, for instance, gradually learns to save his nickel and sacrifice his immediate desires for the sake of some future good—the purchase of a pet, for example. The young man, the night before a critical business interview, chooses the long-range value of study and rest against the passing pleasure of a post-theatre cocktail party. When we are dedicated to a cause, we are willing to suffer deprivation, criticism, and even ridicule for the sake of the object of our devotion. In other words, when we are primarily concerned about our security, we need the reassurance of immediate satisfaction and pleasure, and will usually respond to the demands of our feelings. On the other hand, any maturity that we may have achieved will show itself in our ability to keep our eyes on our goals and in our willingness to sacrifice for the long-term purpose.

Second, the mature person is able to accept things and people the way they are, rather than pretend they are the way he wants them to be.

When we were children, we were full of alarms and pretenses. "Are we going to have an accident, Daddy?" asked a child who had just heard her father complain about the traffic and the way some people were driving. Another child pretended to be someone else when she was afraid. This is all right for children since they have to learn the nature of reality and truth by moving back and forth between fantasy and reality, fiction and truth. So in childhood our fears were easily aroused, and we loved to make-believe.

But now that we are more grown-up, such confusions between fantasy and reality, fiction and truth, are most unfortunate, for they render us incapable of any kind of responsible role or relationship in life. For the sake of a false sense of security, we attempt to see things as we wish they were. Wishing to be secure, a woman pretends that her husband still loves her, despite all evidence to the contrary. At the same time, her fears blind her to the strengths and resources in herself and in her situation, and cause her to do foolish things. It is the same story with the man who, because of his general insecurity with other people, becomes unduly anxious about the irritations that his wife expresses. He sees his relationship with her as worse than it is.

The more mature we are, the more we are able to see things as they are and to act accordingly. We do not have to deal in blacks or whites, and thus misrepresent the nature of life. We may see dangers, but we also see opportunities. We may see evil, but we also see good. In other words, along with seeing the problems, we are able to see, and to use, our resources.

Third, the mature person is able to accept the authority of others without the rebellion or without the self-abdication that we call "folding up."

When we are immature and seeking security as an end in itself, we are likely to be excessively dependent and to express this dependence by a defiance of authority. We may find it difficult to accept advice because of an overwhelming need to appear self-sufficient. We will want to be the big boss and run our own and other people's lives. Our attitude toward our parents, policemen, the boss, government, or other authorities, may be one of ever-ready, armed defensiveness, manifesting itself, in all likelihood, in resentment, if not in outright hostility. A part of the same pattern, however, is that we often rush to positions of authority, such as officer of an organization, teacher, or minister, in order to exercise in relation to others the authority we ourselves cannot accept. We also may do a great deal of talking about the importance of authority and how, without it, society falls apart. Hierarchies, bureaucracies, and organizations of all kinds include a large number of people of this sort, and it is they who are responsible for the worst sins of these organizations.

On the other hand, as we move from our security preoccupations to our maturity occupations, we can accept authority more easily. We can take orders, if need be, without resentment. We can accept correction in good grace. We are able to learn from our mistakes. Our respect for law and order provides a basis for reverence and, therefore, a capacity for love and worship. The truly devout person is one who is obedient to the nature of life and lives in a disciplined relation to it.

Fourth, the mature person is one who is able to accept himself as an authority without either a sense of bravado or a sense of guilt.

When we are excessively dependent because of our immaturity, we cannot make decisions without consulting endless numbers of people. When we receive help, we are embarrassed that we have had to accept it, and may quite conveniently forget to give thanks. If things go wrong, we are likely to blame other people. We may find it difficult to exercise comfortably the authority that goes with our role as husband, wife, parent, or whatever. Our insecurity may cause our authority to be inconsistent or tyrannical. On the other hand, when we act with authority, we may have overwhelming feelings of guilt about having to act so decisively and directly. For these reasons, many of us cannot be depended upon to carry out our responsibilities. At one time we are overly strict; at another, overly lenient. We use our authority to bolster and reinforce personal insecurity. Or, our personal insecurity betrays us into a leniency that keeps us from doing what we need to do. It may even make us feel so guilty about taking a clear and strong position that we very rarely do so.

As we advance from security preoccupations to maturity occupations, we become able to accept our own and others' authority. We can take advice and give it. We can make our own decisions. We can give help and accept help with equal pleasure and gratitude. If our enterprises fail, we can sort out our own and others' responsibilities for the failure, learn from our mistakes, and pick ourselves up to start over again. We are more able to respect ourselves, love our brothers, and worship God.

Fifth, a mature person is able to defend himself both from his own unacceptable impulses and from attacks from the outside.

We all have impulses, attitudes, and ideas that make us feel guilty and that interfere with our relations to others. When we experience these impulses, we have to choose a method of dealing with them. Sometimes the method we choose is not a mature one. When we feel guilty about hostile feelings toward someone, we may criticize ourselves violently and, in an exaggerated fashion, tear ourselves down. It is as if we were trying to make atonement for our offense and achieve a feeling of being forgiven. This method of dealing with our hostile impulses is unsatisfactory because it does not help us. It does not lead to constructive solutions, and it makes it more difficult for other people to live with us.

Another common method of defense against what we do

not like in ourselves is scapegoating, that is, blaming others instead of ourselves. Rather than accept our responsibility for failure, we place it on someone else. If we can make them seem to be responsible, then we do not have to do anything about the situation ourselves. Thus, we gain a false and spurious sense of security and well-being. This is the case when a man, having difficulty in his business affairs, blames his associates for the situation, and thus saves himself from having to face unpleasant truths about himself.

In contrast to this kind of defense, when mature, we face frankly the truth about ourselves and deal with our conflicts without too much disturbance. We are better able to exercise self-control if that seems to be indicated; or to make some form of renunciation in order to choose another good; or to undertake to change the circumstances of our lives in ways that will help us to live more harmoniously and productively. We may even direct the energy of our troublesome impulses into channels that are creative and acceptable. Many people turn to arts, crafts, hobbies, or games as a way of expressing creatively feelings that have been produced by frustration. Instead of rebelling destructively, they turn their rebellion into beauty, usefulness, and recreation.

We also need to be able to defend ourselves from outside attacks: from criticisms, both justified and unjustified, from slander, and from being made the scapegoat of other people's failures. When we are immature, our response to these attacks can be so emotional that we lose ability to judge the situation rightly, and are betrayed into unwise action to the injury of our relationships with others. On the other hand, a mature response enables us to evaluate the nature of the attack. If it is justifiable criticism, we consider the source and accept it. We are able to do the appropriate thing in relation to what other people say and do. We can get angry without feeling guilty about it, and if the situation calls for righteous indignation, we do not have to justify it. We even have some power to ignore injury if that seems to be the thing to do. When it is necessary for us to take the initiative in speaking to the person whose behavior has caused the injury, we are better able to do that, too. In other words, the mature person is sufficiently secure as to be able to conduct himself with the minimum of alarm in the inevitable vicissitudes of living.

Sixth, the mature person is able to work without being a slave, and to play without feeling that he ought to be working.

Because of our immaturity, we work as if we were God —that is, we work as if everything depended upon us. Because of insecurity, we work with anxiety and without stopping. When we are not working, we feel guilty. When we are working, we do so without a sense of accomplishment and well-being. We comment frequently on how hard we are working or, in other ways, draw attention to the fact that we are working.

Moreover, because of our immaturity, we are not able to play any more than are we able to work. Perhaps the best way to characterize our play is to say that we play as if the play were work. While we play, we often feel that we should be back on the job. The result is that our play is not re-creating, is not recreation. Because of our attitude toward work, we are likely to be over-anxious about money, which, instead of being a means, becomes an end. And in our play, we either spend our money too recklessly, or feel guilty about spending any at all.

On the other hand, when we are able to give ourselves to life more maturely, we have a healthy sense of responsibility and give ourselves to our work more gladly. Yet, we refuse to allow ourselves to become slaves to our work, and can distinguish between ourselves and our work. At appropriate times we can detach ourselves from work and, with a sense of release and liberation, give ourselves to recreation. In other words, we are able to work when we work, and play when we play. And we do not confuse the two. We draw a sense of fulfillment from our work, even when it may not seem to offer much in that direction.

Seventh, a mature person is one who is able to accept his own, and the opposite, sex and the relation between the two in ways that are appropriately fulfilling.

It is important for a man to be happy because he is a man, and for a woman to be happy because she is a woman. When this is the case, there is less difficulty in the relation between the sexes. The immature person is one who is insecure in his sex role. There are men who often want to reject the masculine role, not only in their sexual life but in life in general. Of course, the rejection by women of their role is more frequent because, in our culture, social and economic forces favor them less, and greater fears are associated with being a woman.

The more mature we are, the more we are able to recognize that men have certain qualities and assets that women do not have, and women some that men do not have. Each of us rejoices in what he is and has, and looks for his complement in the other.

As we mature, our sex impulse becomes more genitalized and is not diverted or deviated into satisfactions that are exhibitionistic, sadistic, masochistic, and dependent upon fantasies or focused upon any other part of the body or upon other things. We look for sexual satisfaction through coitus in a permanent and responsible partnership. According to this concept, promiscuity is a sign of immaturity and a symptom of insecurity.

This concept might seem to exclude the unmarried. Certainly those who are unwillingly single would seem to be penalized by it. But some things need to be made clear at this point. First, sexual maturity does not necessarily mean sexual activity. The unmarried person or one who practices continency may be just as mature as any married person. Nor does it follow that married people and/or the sexually active are for that reason mature. As we have suggested above, we work for relationships that are appropriately fulfilling. In whatever state we find ourselves, married or single, we can come closer to the adequacy suitable to that state.

Thus, the mature sexual person is also one capable of a relationship with the opposite sex without the necessity of a physical relationship. They are capable of a sincere friendship without sexual involvement. The immature person is one who cannot think of a relationship between man and woman in other than a physical or sexual sense. Obviously, such people will encounter great difficulty in their relationships with others, and will cause a great deal of heartache in any marriage they may undertake.

Eighth, the mature person is one who is able to love others so satisfyingly that he becomes less dependent upon being loved.

Our immaturity reveals us as persons, who, because of insecurity, are on the constant lookout for people to love us. We are in constant need of reassurance that we are loved. Indeed, we may be so busy asking for love that we are unable to love. For us, then, love can only be a feeling, a romance, a sentiment. We will think of love as primarily receiving. When we are called upon to give in a love relationship, we regard giving as demand, deprivation, or as an injustice which arouses our resentment. We engage in a great deal of self-love and are constantly preoccupied with our own well-being. Even though we want love most desperately, we may be afraid to accept it when it is offered. These responses on our part inevitably discourage the love-offerings of others so that our state becomes progressively worse, unless somehow we can be reached by a love that has the power to heal us.

On the other hand, when we have moved from our security preoccupations to our maturity occupations, we find that it is more blessed to give than to receive. For us, love is now action expressed in terms of our responsibility for others. When we give love, we feel strengthened and renewed. We are singularly unaware of the measurements of love received or given and, according to the degree of our maturity, have the power to love without expecting it to be returned, or being affected too adversely by the absence of it. Our love enables us to break through the barriers which separate us from others. *Whereas the immature loses love by seeking it, the mature person produces love by loving.* The immature person who is preoccupied by his need of being loved is lonely. The person who loves is blessed with varied and rich relationships.

The love of our enemy is perhaps the most mature expression of love. It does not mean that we approve of, or surrender to, him. Rather, it means that while protecting ourselves, we try to be responsible for him. Hatred of the enemy, personal or national, misguides us, and may even make us more vulnerable to injury. Love of our enemy makes us more responsible for him, for ourselves, and for all our relationships upon which our safe deliverance ultimately depends.

Ninth and finally, the mature person is one who is able to accept his significant place and role in the larger scheme of things.

The immature person, out of his insecurity and anxiety, tries to be the center of his universe—often without knowing what he is doing. He tries to be God, as it were, and tries to order all things according to his own pleasure and will.

We show our maturity by our respect for others, by our listening to them. We can live with others and participate in common enterprises. We can rejoice in another's ability and success without feeling that our ability and achievements are diminished. Furthermore, we do not have to work for immediate rewards. We are capable of living and serving, and leaving the ultimate issues of life in the hands of One who is the Source and End of life. The highly developed and responsible person is one who has faith in God; and because he has this faith in God, he has faith in man and in himself.

These, then, are some of the criteria of maturity. In our discussion of them we have tried to show how essential it is to move from the earlier preoccupations of childhood to the maturity occupations of the adult. For only as we succeed in this, can we hope to meet our personal social, political, and religious problems and opportunities.

Some readers, especially those with a theological orientation, may raise, however, the following question about these criteria: Are you not suggesting, they will ask, that by the achievement of maturity—assuming that it is even relatively achievable—man *can* save himself? My answer to this question is: Yes, one can read that view into any effort toward maturity; indeed, many people work toward achieving maturity with the clear assumption in mind that they *can* save themselves. The Christian, however, may use these criteria without holding to that assumption. In fact, he will use them with a quite different view in mind, one compatible with his acknowledgment of dependence on Christ as Saviour. For, in using these criteria, he will ever be humbly aware that human perfectibility is severely limited and is, in fact, dependent upon the help and grace of God through Christ; and that in ordering his thoughts and feelings through discussions such as we have been holding together, he is only taking a step toward opening himself to God's help and grace through Christ; and, finally, that his achievement of maturity to whatever degree will be the work of that grace and help.

While, then, we cannot save ourselves in the ultimate sense, we can live responsibly and responsively as men with men. Accordingly, there remains for us to determine who is to give us the immediate help we need in this growth. What is the source of the security that is so necessary if we are to accept our responsibilities courageously?

As we have already said, we enter life completely dependent and in need of the ministry of others to get a start. This means that we are dependent upon our homes, our schools, our churches, and all other cultural influences that have responsibility for us. Their faith, their view of life, their attitude toward us, and the kind of love they give us are determinative. Our experience of trust and love provides us with the basic security; and with this heritage, we are better able to face with courage whatever life may bring us. And it is through the power of the personal, as interpreted in an earlier chapter, that we receive the heritage of security that enables us to move toward maturity.

10

A Faith for the Middle Years

"*I wonder if our minister really believes in God? If he did, he might have the courage to face what's going on in the world and try to throw some light on it. Come to think of it, we've got to go to a meeting at the church tonight. Money for another building. Our church costs us a lot of money and time. Julie says that if you don't put a lot in a thing, you don't get much out. . . . Wonder what would happen if I raised the questions at tonight's meeting: Why raise more money for another building? What's the church doing to justify its present outlay? What's the purpose of the Church, anyway? . . . I can't do it —it would raise too much of a stink.*"

—Dick Foster

10 Dick Foster, we find, has been doing some hard thinking about himself, his marriage, his children, his work, and the purpose of his life. Like others in their middle years, he has been reassessing his values, weighing them, discarding the ones that have turned out to be false, and trying to understand and hold on to the ones that are true. He wants to determine what values and goals are worthy of his attention and effort. And in his middle years, it is more important than ever for him to know what can be dispensed with and what he should keep and build on for the rest of his life.

Dick Foster senses, as do many in their middle years, that he now has a second chance to live his life with more meaning and purpose, and to prevent his later years from being empty and miserable. For the middle years can be a time of synthesis, a time for drawing from the life that has been lived meaning for the life that yet awaits us.

i

In their middle years people are often thought to be conservative and reactionary. They can be, of course, but what is sometimes wrongly interpreted as conservatism is a deliberateness and thoughtfulness. By this time they are beginning to achieve a balance between activity and contemplation. They are no longer so interested in running around and in aimless novelty. The truths that they have found and their relationships with others are becoming more important. They may be questioning what their faith and beliefs really are; they may be searching for a faith by which to live.

As we look back over the discussion in the preceding chapters, some insights that can contribute to a faith for the middle years have come to light. One central insight is the importance of being able to give ourselves to one another. The meaning of life opens to the person who can give himself to it; to the person who is able to commit himself to his wife, to his children, to his friends, to his work, to his responsibilities, to God. In the beginning of our life we are the recipients of its gifts; but in its noontime we are the bestowers of its gifts. The life of commitment begins with the act of self-giving and is continued by decisions and actions that express that self-giving over and over again.

We saw in our discussion of marriage how indispensably important the power to give oneself is to the success of the relationship. We saw that marriage is only possible where each partner gives himself to the other with the faith that through that relationship each will be called into fuller being.

We have also seen that this kind of voluntary self-surrender is not easy for us to make, and does not occur as commonly as we may assume. When we try to give ourselves, it is likely to be with reservations. We practice a "I'll-love-you-if" attitude, hoping thereby to avoid the pain of self-giving love. We want a guaranteed return on our love, trust not being a characteristic attitude of our times. We are afraid to love, even afraid to accept love, and yet we know that the answer to personal vulnerability and insecurity is in the relationship of love that calls for self-commitment. But this withholding of ourselves impairs the very relationships so necessary for life, such as marriage and parenthood. For this inability and failure to give ourselves freely produces anxiety in us. Our real anxiety, however, stems not from our relationship to the world of nature, but from our relationship to the world of persons. In the exploration and harnessing of nature we as a people have been outstandingly successful, but we have not been so successful in living our personal relations. Our knowledge and power frighten us when we realize that, because of the character of our relationships, we cannot trust ourselves and others in the use of such knowledge and power. As we have seen, there can be no security without trust, and without security one dares not trust. Love can only be found through self-surrender, but self-surrender is only possible where there is love. This is our predicament. Although the meaning of our lives can only be found in our relationship with others, we still do not really trust those relationships. The answer to our predicament, then, is a faith that will help us to give ourselves to these relationships despite our not feeling quite safe in doing so.

Obviously, our discussion has now moved into the realm of religion, and we are talking about the religious life. But even religion cannot be trusted since it has often led men to deny life, to withdraw from the claims and the needs of men, and with dogmatic arrogance to hide from the sight of others the face of God. We are always having to be brought back to "true religion." In His day Christ found much religious organization and leadership opposed to Him and deaf to the cries of people. The same is true now, unfortunately. Yet our greatest teachers today point out that Christ came to save men from the enslavement of moralistic, legalistic religion. And the Bible through the Prophets and the New Testament tells us that God's call comes to us through personal encounter, that He speaks to men through individuals and whole peoples. Biblical history is the story of God's action through men.

The turning point of this history is in the person of Jesus of Nazareth, who was called Emmanuel, meaning "God with us"—that is, God with us in person-to-person encounter in order that we might be reconciled and reunited with one another in Him. In Jesus, the Christ, we see the Word of

God as the *lived* life of God, which addresses us personally and calls us personally into being. This understanding opens for us the nature and the realm of the call of God. The call is personal, and comes to us through "The Person" and persons. It is the call to commitment, the call to give ourselves.

$$\ddot{i}\dot{i}$$

Since this is the nature of God's call, then our response must be of the same nature. The personal is the realm of His activity, and we must pay attention to the personal if we would hear His voice. If we would respond to Him, we must respond personally in personal relations. Here is the true context for self-giving.

What must this mean? In the first place, it must mean that we can no longer hold the erroneous concept of a separation between the religious and secular worlds. In their religion men have always tended to build walls within which to confine God. They have always tried to make God fit into the little houses they have built for Him. In Christ, God broke out of those bonds into the world and life. But men continue to try to build those walls and to confine God in their doctrines, their denominations, and their forms of worship. A captured God, we think, is safer and more comfortable than God "on the loose." In this way we seek to make Him serve our purposes, and try to make Him feel at home in our life. But we live in the age of the Holy Spirit, who bursts again and again the walls which fearful men build for Him.

We must not think that the men who build thus are necessarily other men. Any one of us is capable of doing it —and we do. When we fail to make the necessary distinction between the truth and our prejudices, when we try to line God up on the side of our prejudice as if it were His truth, we are not open to what God has to say to us. The result is that we take our prejudice, whether it be one with respect to race relations or churchmanship, and use it to beat other men over the head in order to bring them into line with our convictions. But God is too big for our little temples.

The world is the place where God is working out His purposes, and everything that happens in the world has meaning in relation to Him. The world is the arena of His action, and only as we study the meaning of His action in this world, we come to know Him. Thus, everything has religious meaning. We know, therefore, that if we would serve him, we must do so in this world, in its work and in its play, taking seriously its problems and issues, and witnessing for the truth of God wherever and whenever we see its relevance. We cannot retreat from the world to be religious. To be truly religious, we must seek to do God's will in the world.

Second, if God calls us through the personal and our response must be personal, certain changes must take place in our thoughts about each other. No longer can we think of others as objects whom we may direct and use and experience. Dick and Julie Foster have begun to learn this lesson, and are beginning to find each other as persons, in relation to whom they must stand with respect and expectation. Moreover, we can no longer think of ourselves as self-sufficient and independent. Nor should we allow others to think of us as the object of their ambition or desire. While we accept the truth that we have to serve one another out of our respective functions, yet because we are made in the image of God, we respect ourselves and expect others to respect us as persons; and we must, therefore, resist any attempt on anyone's part to exploit us. Others are a part of our life and we are a part of theirs. We also begin to realize that everything we do and are is an expressive sign of the living Word who speaks through us to one another. The thoughtful phone call or note may be more than a sign of our care and consideration; it may be experienced as something much greater than that—for some even as the love of God. So we must learn to think of ourselves as the instrument of the living Word who through us seeks others. Modern psychology has taught us to recognize that everything that happens has meaning. But psychology does not always acknowledge that the meaning of everything points either directly or indirectly to the ultimate meaning. A genuine act of self-sacrifice, however, may restore someone's faith not only in man, but also in God. It does not always happen, but it may happen; and the possibility gives us a clue to the nature of our life and of its relationships. Therefore, we do not look for a religious experience off in the blue, unrelated to life, but rather for one that gives everyday life religious meaning. We do not seek God by closing ourselves to life in order that we might find Him, but by opening ourselves to life in order that He may appear and speak to us and through us.

In the parables of the Last Judgment those who were puzzled as to when they had ministered to the Son of man asked, "When did we see thee sick or in prison and visit thee?" Then He said to them, "Truly as you did it to one of the least of these, my brethren, you did it to me." (*Matt.* 25:37-40) In other words, our service to God is to be seen and recognized in our service to one another, and the truth with which we honor God is not contained in the words of our hymns, prayers and worship only, but in our actions as well.

It is tragic that Dick and Julie Foster expected so little
help from their church, and that their church, including
their minister, Dr. Powers, gave them so little help. As is so
often true, the Church is too concerned with its own institutional life and the external observances of its worship to be
helpfully concerned with people. Dr. Powers was afraid to
face, with Dick and Julie, their problems. For some reason
personal matters made him feel uneasy, and he used the
church's worship and its activities as a way of keeping
people and their problems at a safe distance. Because he
was afraid of people, he was unable to help them. Other
ministers fortunately are able to practice, as well as preach
about, the love that is primarily concerned with persons and
their needs. They lead the Church in the exercise of responsible love which seeks to reunite men. Reuniting love is
not concerned whether people are right or wrong, good or
bad, wise or foolish, black or white, Roman Catholic or
Episcopalians or Baptists or Methodists; it is concerned
only that people should be loved and respond to love by
loving.

iii

We are now ready to consider some
aspects of a faith for the mature creative years. This faith
is not aimed at converting people to a point of view, to a
morality, to an institution, or to a set of ideas of propositions. Success in such enterprises may be failure because
their objective is limited and partial and, therefore, idola-
trous. The reason for God's redeeming action, namely
Incarnation in a person, was that He might make His
appeal through persons, and not through dogma or any set
of propositions, or through law or ethics, or through programs. He makes His appeal through Christ, and in making

us members of His body, makes His appeal through us. He calls us by His love through one another, and we respond to Him through one another in love.

As a result of this personal revelation of God, we possess some understandings to guide us in our living. The first applies to our conception and expectation of human nature. We know that the character of human nature is paradoxical. On the one hand, man is but a little lower than God, and is crowned with glory and honor, and under God holds dominion over the beasts and the whole world of nature. (See *Psalm* 8:4-8.) On the other hand, man is "like unto the beasts that perish." That he dies is the outward and visible sign of the inner corruption of his nature. The great philosophers of all ages have generally agreed with this fundamental biblical perception of man's paradoxical nature. Pascal referred to man as at once "the glory and scum of the universe." The Bible knows both man's wretchedness and his high destiny.

When we stop to think about it, we realize from our own experience how true the biblical insight is. This double truth about ourselves was a stumbling block to Dick and Julie as it is to many of us. At one time, we respond joyously to every true and good call and impulse, and then we are appalled at the hatefulness and wickedness of which we can be capable. Therefore, we should have no illusions about ourselves and others. We expect people to be good, and we expect them to be evil. Because we know our own frailty, we try not to judge others too harshly, and because we can see the traces of the image of God in us, we try not to despair about our own and others' frailty and sin.

Second, we believe that the relationships of love—marriage, family, friendship—are more important than any other human values; and that nothing—money, fame, things, pride, being right, or anything else—is more important than an open, communicating, loving relationship with one another. For this reason Dick and Julie are accepting the pain of communication for the sake of a new relationship. Love, they are discovering, is the source, the energy, and the objective of their life. But love cannot be initiated or possessed by either of them alone; it can only be found between them. Without this betweenness, this relationship, this love, is impossible. We were given the new relationship by God in order that we might find love, a love that would forgive and possess us. Since God wills to meet us in relationship, Dick and Julie must expect to find Him as they continue to seek each other and work out their relationship. Since His Word is incarnate, the words that we use must also be incarnate. To put it another way, God's Word was incarnate in Jesus living the life of perfect love. And so the words they would use must also be incarnate, that is, love expressed in their actions, in their mutual repentance, and in their forgiveness of each other. And *our* faith must be translated into action. We need to use both the language of words and the language of relationship.

Third, we believe that the personal meaning and action of our faith must find expression in community, and this is what we should mean by the Church. The Church, in part, is a community of people living acceptingly in response to love. If Dick and Julie had known the Church as such a community of responsible love, their story might have been different. The Church, when it is true to its calling, is to be found in the world doing the work of God, seeking the truth, loving the unloved, wrestling with the forces of evil, living with all men as children of God. It is when we are doing these things that we are the Church acting; but that cannot be said about us when we have retreated from the world and are babbling about the *insular* matters of religion, and wastefully consuming the energies of the Church members in *inconsequential* work and activity.

The Church is an army that has been sent on a mission. In order to accomplish its purpose, it must have a base; and in order for it to have a base, it assigns certain troops the task of building and maintaining the base so that the rest of the army may be free to do its job! We tend, however, to forget the Church's mission and wastefully assign most of our people to building and maintaining "bases" with the result that we do not accomplish its true purpose. More members need to be assigned to, and trained for, the true work out in the world, where the conflict between life and death goes on unceasingly.

The purpose of the Church is not to serve itself, but to be the redeeming community. The community exists in order that those who do not know Christ may find Him through relationship with His people. The Church is the personal community that exists to give expression to the revelation of the meaning of the personal and of love. It is the community from which we should expect the greatest manifestation of the power of the personal.

The Church is necessary to salvation because God's revelation of Himself is personal and requires a community of persons for its communication. When we become a part of that community, we begin to receive and communicate the revelation. In our coming together, God comes to us. This is according to the promise: "When two or three are gathered together in my name, there am I in the midst of them." Thus the Church is the basic structure given us by God for a life of faith in which we and Dick and Julie may find our place.

Fourth, because of the tensions between persons and

things we need a faith that is sacramental. Earlier, in our discussion of the tensions, we found that we both love and use persons. We also saw that our use of one another is made in the context of our regard for one another as persons. If we basically love each other, our use of each other will not destroy the reverence for the person or the possibility of new meetings in love. We also both love and use things. But if our love of things becomes a substitute for the love of persons, then we are making idols out of them, and our love of them will destroy us. But if we love things as symbols of the personal, such as loving our house because it is our home, then the love of things can be creative.

In other words, things are meant to serve persons. And they have been made instruments of God's act of redemption. Our Lord, on the night before He was betrayed, took bread and wine, and when He had given thanks, said, "This is my body. This is my blood." And He bade us to eat and drink and be restored to unity with Him and one another in the Holy Communion. Here certain things, bread and wine, were made to be outward and visible signs of a new relationship. Likewise, all things by this example are meant to be signs and instruments of personal trust, love, and communion.

Because the bread and wine of Holy Communion are manufactured things, in the sense that man has to do something to their basic elements to make them what they are, they may stand for everything that we make, and for our whole economic enterprise. Therefore, since our Lord used bread and wine to be the external sign of His love and life, it is implicit in His act that all manufactured things may be expressive instruments of love and life. In this way, the sacrament of the Holy Communion speaks to the way in which persons possess and use the things that men make. The lovely furnishings of the home, for instance, should contribute to the quality of family life and be sacraments of that relationship. Instead, our property concerns are often a common cause of conflict between persons. According to this sacramental principle, such results of man's creativity as supersonic flight and modern means of communication should also be outward and visible signs, effective instruments, of the achievement of community in which men become related as persons rather than a means of destruction. The relation of persons and things is meant to be a mutually creative relation rooted in the love of God.

Finally, the only faith worth having is a ministering faith, one that empowers us to give ourselves in love and service to others. The word "ministry," however, is unfortunately associated with the work of ordained ministers, so that lay people do not characteristically think of themselves as ministers. The word "layman," according to popular usage, refers to those who are either ignorant or amateurs. This is true not only in the field of religion, but also in that of science. The Church's influence in the world has been greatly enfeebled by the existence of this erroneous concept. The number of ordained Protestant ministers in America is small as compared to the number of people who need the Ministry of the Church. If the former constitute the whole Ministry of the Church, as many people think, the work of the Church is dependent upon a pathetically small group. As long as the work of the ministry is confined to what ordained ministers can do, the Ministry of the Church will be weak and unequal to its task.

The whole Ministry of the Church is the work of all its people. God chose a people through whom He might make His claim and in order that the Divine Love might express itself through men living and working together as the community of God, set in the midst of the broken lives of men; that worship of Him might reveal the meaning of daily events and provide guidance for historical decisions; and that His work of reuniting hostile and separated men might be carried on everywhere where men live, work, love, and play. Every individual whether ordained or not, is God's person living in relation to persons. Whoever accepts that relation responsibly is a minister.

Under the UNESCO program, for example, something like five to seven million people in Indonesia have been cured of that miserable disease, the yaws, and given a new life. How should Christians view this tremendous work of healing, and the men and women who carry it out? Some have not known about it and others are grateful that their government is humanitarian. But how many of us church people recognize this healing of millions of people as an expression of the healing of Christ and the workers as his ministers? When we do not so view such work, we are allowing it to become separated from its source in the Christian spirit. We protest the secularization of life and try to place the blame for it on the modern world. Actually, the secular is caused by modern religious man when he confines his religion to religion, that is, to church activities, observances, and practices without seeing that religion's main concern is for all of life.

When young men or women go into UNESCO service, to continue the example, or into any other service for that matter, we should recognize them and help them to recognize themselves as ministers of Christ and as participants in the Church's ministry. And the Churches should pray for them and keep in touch with them, receiving and sharing reports on their work, and thanking God that it was out of the spirit of Christ in the world that this work of theirs was quickened and begun.

In this sense all service may be gathered up as the work of God, all men may have a ministry, and the kingdom of the secular beaten back by the Kingdom of God which claims all work and all men. In this concept the ordained minister, in addition to his priestly responsibilities, is the leader and trainer of people for their ministry. He is the pastor of pastors, the teacher of teachers, the minister of ministers.

As Dick and Julie Foster began to discover that they had such a ministry and learned to practice it, they made great strides in meeting their own difficulties. In the first place, their very struggle against their own separation and distress made them more aware of the same travail in others. Second, the inspiration and example of George Duncan in helping their daughter Jane taught them much about the power of people to help one another. Ordinarily, neither they nor he would have thought of George Duncan as God's minister of healing, but whoever does His healing work is His servant. This was Christ's attitude, for He told His disciples who questioned the work of someone who was not a follower of Jesus, "Do not forbid him, for he that is not against us is for us." (Luke 9:50) And third, Dick and Julie, with the rest of us have work to do that may help others. For example, this is a time of widespread loneliness because people are on the move with no time to put down roots. Parents are alone in raising their children because they no longer have common values and attitudes from which they might gather support. Cocktail parties are filled with people whose hearts are breaking with the longing for real companionship. Not only do we all share in this universal loneliness, but we see it in others to whom we ourselves may minister. We gain strength, however, for our own struggles when we help others with theirs. Indeed, our own flagging courage is renewed whenever we give courage to the other fellow. And the power of our love is increased the more we give love. The prescription for a lonely person is for him to seek out and comfort another lonely person.

The middle years are a time when we have a second chance for individual change and growth. The experience of these years may be like that of adolescence in terms of character transformations and the discovery of new capacities. It can be a time for developing interests and talents that are enriching. Almost everyone has some one thing that he has wanted to do or become but has allowed the pressure of time and responsibility to crowd it out. The middle years can be the time when we begin to do and be those things, and thus recover and acquire some of our potential creativity.

Personality develops through the exercise of responsibility for one another and the conditions of our life. We cannot become creative and mature persons without living in a widening circle of interaction with our fellowmen. In Christ all people become neighbors, one to another. In today's world "neighbor" includes among others, buyers and sellers, workers and bosses, teachers and pupils, doctors and patients, Russians and Americans, black and white, East and West. As followers of Christ, we recognize that every human being has claim upon us. Because these years bring us a deepening of values and a second chance to realize them, we may be more ready to give ourselves to God and man in this ministry of love and service. Thus we who are in our middle years are called by both God and man to responsible action for our neighbors. Will we hear and give ourselves?

If, out of the travail of living, we can bring understanding, love, and care to the lives of others, we know that our middle years have become, indeed, our creative years.

SUGGESTED READINGS

SUGGESTED READINGS

Chapter 2

Paul Tournier. *The Meaning of Persons*. New York: Harper & Bros., 1957.

Pamphlets:

"The Modern Mother's Dilemma" by Sidonie M. Gruenberg and Hilda S. Krech, Public Affairs Pamphlets, 22 E. 38th St., New York 16, N.Y.

"Self-understanding: a first step to understanding children" by William C. Menninger, M.D. Spencer Press, Inc., Chicago, Ill., 1951.

Chapter 3

Martin Buber. *Between Man and Man*. New York: Macmillan & Company, 1955. Boston: Beacon Press, paperback edition.

Brewster Ghiselin. *The Creative Process:* A Symposium. New York: New American Library, 1955.

Chapter 4

Smiley Blanton. *Love or Perish*. New York: Simon & Schuster, 1956.

Erich Fromm. *The Art of Loving*. New York: Harper & Bros., 1956.

Ashley Montagu. *The Meaning of Love*. New York: The Julian Press, Inc., 1953.

Vladimir Solovyev. *The Meaning of Love*. New York: International Universities Press, 1946.

Chapter 5

Simon Doniger, Editor. *Sex and Religion Today*. New York: Association Press. 1953.

W. Norman Pittenger. *The Christian View of Sexual Behavior.*
New York: Seabury Press, 1954.

Pamphlets:

"The Christian View of Sex" by Hugh C. Warner. SCM Press,
Ltd., 56 Bloomsbury Street, London, England.

"Sexual Harmony in Marriage" by Oliver M. Butterfield.
Emerson Books, Inc., 251 W. 19th St., New York 11, 1953.

Chapter 6

David R. Mace. *Whom God Hath Joined.* Philadelphia: The
Westminster Press, 1953.

Anne Proctor. *Background to Marriage* or The First Twenty
Years. New York: Longmans, Green, 1953.

Pamphlet:

"Building Your Marriage" by Evelyn Millis Duvall. Public
Affairs Pamphlet No. 113.

Chapter 7

Marynia F. Farnham. *The Adolescent.* New York: Harper &
Bros., 1951.

John Charles Wynn. *How Christian Parents Face Family Problems.* Philadelphia: The Westminster Press, 1955.

Pamphlets:

"Democracy Begins in the Home" by Ernest Osborne. Public
Affairs Pamphlet No. 192.

"Guiding the Adolescent" Federal Security Agency, Social Security Administration, Children's Bureau, Publication 225. Re-
vised 1946. Superintendent of Documents, U.S. Government
Printing Office, Washington 25, D.C.

"How to Live with Children" Edith G. Neisser. Spencer Press,
Inc., Chicago, Ill., 1950.

"Let's Listen to Youth" H. H. Remmers & C. G. Hackett.
Science Research Associates, 57 W. Grand Ave., Chicago 10, Ill.

"Making the Grade as Dad" Walter and Edith Neisser. Public Affairs Pamphlet No. 157.

Chapter 8

Stephen S. Bayne, Jr. *Christian Living.* New York: Seabury Press, 1957.

Robert Lowry Calhoun. *God and the Day's Work.* New York: Association Press, 1943.

Alexander Miller. *Christian Faith and My Job.* New York: Association Press, 1946.

Elton Trueblood. *Your Other Vocation.* New York: Harper & Bros., 1952.

Chapter 9

Rollo May. *Man's Search for Himself.* New York: W. W. Norton & Company, Inc., 1953.

Chapter 10

Emil Brunner. *Misunderstanding of the Church.* Philadelphia: The Westminster Press, 1953.

David E. Roberts. *The Grandeur and Misery of Man.* New York: Oxford University Press, 1955.

Lewis Joseph Sherrill. *The Struggle of the Soul.* New York: The Macmillan Company, 1951.

Pamphlet:

"Laymen's Work" No. 8, Special Issue, Spring 1955. World Council of Churches, Geneva, Switzerland. *See* articles: "The Nature of the Church"; "Adult Christianity."

INDEX

INDEX

Acceptance: and the power of the personal, 35-40; *see* Love, work of

Adolescence: and acceptance, 30; and the accepting community, 35; changed expression of love in, 153-54; keeping communication open during, 158-59; and conflict, 143-44; help from outside home, 154-57; influences outside home, 141-42; and loneliness, 29; and parental guilt and anxiety, 145-46; parental mistakes during, 140-41; parental problems during, 140; parental resources for period of, 151-52; sexual relationship, 33-34; and role of family and community, 29-30; security in, 195-96; and self authority, 159-60

Adolescents: achievement of independence, 138-39; achievement of maturity, 136; changes in methods of handling, 142-43; effect of heredity and environment on, 148-49; life choices, 134; parents' acceptance of, 147-48; and parental resistances, 136-38; their problems, 134-39; their resistances, 135-39; self reliance, 134; sexual development, 135; withdrawal, 134

Authority and maturity, 200-01

Bible, 215; and pattern for living together, 116

Brauer, Charles, 168-69

Church, the, 221-22

Commitment: *see* Love

Community, 35

Compatibility, 121-24

Conformity, 192-94

Creativity, 42-61; and healing, 55; illustrated, 44-47; and our life together, 43-44; and machines, 172; and marriage: *see* Marriage; recovery of, 54; risk of, 49-50; and the relationship of love, 59-61; and single-heartedness, 57-58; and techniques, 54; and tensions, 60-61; and the use of things, 58-59

Duncan, George, 45-48

Environment: *see* Heredity

Faith for the middle years, 213-27; and the Church, 221-22; and community, 221; insights for, 213-16; and ministry, 224-26; nature of, 219-20; and the personal, 216; and the relationship of love, 220-21; and personal response, 217-19; and sacraments, 222-24

Foster, Jane, 44-48; transition from adolescence, 51-52

Freedom and love, 84

God, 150; His purpose, 217-18

Growth, nature of personal, 144-45

Heredity and environment, 148-49

Hobbies, 176

Holy Communion, 222-24

Jesus, 215-16; 221; His love, 124; His withdrawal, 28; and the work of love, 72

Juvenile delinquency, 192

Lampert, E., 97

Last Judgment, 218

Life, 168

Listening, 74-75

Love: changes in the expression of, 153-54; and commitment, 72; and freedom, 84; in maturity, 206-07; and the possibility of change, 85-86; four principles of, 101-07; not ready-made, 71-72; and response, 75-79; and romance, 71; tested, 71

Love, the work of, 65-86; and acceptance, 79-81; in action, 65-67, 73; and acts of alienation, 70; and attitudes of fear and resentment, 69-70; and belief, 81-82; and disbelief, 82; giving and receiving, 68; and Jesus, 72; and listening, 74-75; and the middle years, 70-72; and natural separation, 68-69; and reconciliation, 73; and relationship, 69; superficial conception of, 68

Man: biblical conception of, 220

Marriage, 214; affirmations about, 112-29; and boredom, 113-14; after children leave, 126-28; and compatibility, 121-24; creative, 111-29; differences of partners, 119-21; dialogue in, 117; and expectation, 111-12; and giving of self, 114-15; relationship in, 115-19; as a school, 128-29; and time, 125-28

Maturity: and acceptance of self, 201-02; and the acceptance of authority, 200-01; achievement of, 196-97; Christian, 208-09; definition of, 197; guides of, 198-209; long term purposes, 198-99; and love, 206-07; and perspective, 208; and realism, 199-200; and self defense, 202-04; in the sex relationship, 205-06; in work and play, 204-05

Middle years: and change and growth, 227; conservatism in, 213; religion in, 215

Minister, ordained, 224

Orgasm, simultaneous, 106

Parental love: self-denying, 150-51

Parental responsibility, 133-34; to adolescent, 157-63; and the exercise of authority, 160-63; resources of, 151-52; and understanding, 157-58

Parents: creative function of, 150; and changing methods of child rearing, 142-43; and the changing relationship in adolescence, 144-45

Person: our image of, 51; and loneliness, 29; process of becoming a, 26-27; process of becoming in adolescents, 27-28; process of becoming in children, 27

Personal, the power of the, 21-40; and acceptance, 26, 35-40; and anxiety, 24; and competition, 26; and creativity, 48-49, 53; defined, 21; and faith, 38-40; ignorance of, 22-23; and illusions, 38; illustrated, 21-22; and job anxiety, 25; and love and hate, 37; and resentments, 37; vs. technical, 23; and work, 176-79

Prodigal Son, 124-25

Real self, 117-19

Recreation, 204-05

Responsibility: and love, 75-79; and marriage, 99-100; and maturity, 78-79; trust and mistrust, 69-70; withdrawal from, 27-28

Resurrection, 85

Saving Person, 54-55

Security: concerns, 194-95; preoccupation with, 192-94; and technics, 193

Self-surrender, 214

Separation of religious and secular, 216-17

Sex, 33-34

Sex in love, role of, 89-108; and accepting, 103-04; and adolescents, 94; and children, 93-94; and divine love, 100; in times of disillusionment, 99; and expectation, 105-08; and human need, 96-97; and listening, 101; and perfect love, 98; and lust, 98; and marriage, 93; and maturity, 205-06; problem or blessing, 107; procreative function, 92-93; reason for, 90-91; the recreative function, 92; as resource in marriage, 92; and responsibility, 104-05; source of meaning, 95-96

Sexual intercourse, premarital, 93
Sexual relationship: holy, 108
Sleeping Beauty, 60

Things, as instruments of communication, 59

UNESCO, 225
Unfaithfulness, 82-83

Vocation, 31-32

Withdrawal: and creativity, 53; see Relationship

Work, 204-05; attitudes toward conditions of, 171; and the Bible, 171; correcting attitudes toward, 176-83; correcting conditions of, 183-88; and frustration, 167-68; and God, 180-83; of housewives, 181; and maturity, 177-78; meaning of, 168; mechanization of, 172; and middle years, 167-88; moral ambiguity of, 173; and motive, 169-70; and perspective, 181-83; and reconciliation of commitments, 173-75; and its results, 175-76; social necessity of, 179; unrealistic conception of, 170

Youth, work of, 31; from dependence to responsibility, 31-32; nature of change from childhood to adulthood, 31